FREEMEN, FREEHOLDERS, AND CITIZEN SOLDIERS

An Organizational History of Colonel Jonathan Bagley's Regiment,

1755–1760

Brenton C. Kemmer

HERITAGE BOOKS
2011

HERITAGE BOOKS
AN IMPRINT OF HERITAGE BOOKS, INC.

Books, CDs, and more—Worldwide

For our listing of thousands of titles see our website
at
www.HeritageBooks.com

Published 2011 by
HERITAGE BOOKS, INC.
Publishing Division
100 Railroad Ave. #104
Westminster, Maryland 21157

Copyright © 1997 Brenton C. Kemmer

Other books by Brenton C. Kemmer:

Redcoats, Yankees, and Allies:
A History of Uniforms, Clothing, and Gear of the British
Army in the Lake George–Lake Champlain Corridor, 1755–1760

So, Ye Want to be a Reenactor? A Living History Handbook
Brenton C. Kemmer and Karen L. Kemmer

War, Hell and Honor: A Novel of the French and Indian War

The Partisans: Second in a Series of Novels of the French and Indian War

Capture and Redemption: Third in a Series of Novels of the French and Indian War

Through the Eyes of the Bay Colony: The Story of the Involvement of
Massachusetts-Bay in the Battle of Ticonderoga, 1758

All rights reserved. No part of this book may be reproduced or transmitted in any form or by any means, electronic or mechanical, including photocopying, recording or by any information storage and retrieval system without written permission from the author, except for the inclusion of brief quotations in a review.

International Standard Book Numbers
Paperbound: 978-0-7884-0620-1
Clothbound: 978-0-7884-8975-4

CONTENTS:

Acknowledgments i

Part I: "Freemen, Freeholders, and Citizen Soldiers"
    1. Historical involvement in the War 1
    2. History of Jonathan Bagley 5
    3. Demographics of the Regiment 7

Part II: "This Day *NO RUM*"
    4. Recruitment 15
    5. Wages 17
    6. Rations 19

Part III: "An Appearance of Uniformity"
    7. Uniform and equipment, 1755 27
    8. Uniform and equipment, 1756 33
    9. Uniform and equipment, 1757 36
    10. Uniform and equipment, 1758 37
    11. Uniform and equipment, 1759 39
    12. Uniform and equipment, 1760 48

Part IV: "Our duty is so hard that our men scarcely have time to cook their victuals or wash their clothes."
    13. Carpenters and labor 51
    14. Training, drill, and exercise 52
    15. Medicines, ailments, and doctors 53

Part V: "Provisions or the four pence in Leu of it."
    16. Women camp followers 55

Part VI: "When I get out of their power I shall take care how I get in again."
    17. Religion 59
    18. Disobedience and grumbling 59

Appendix 1:
    Range of Age for Soldiers, Bagley's Regiment, 1756 65
Appendix 2:
    Facsimile Officer's Commission 66
Appendix 3:
    Facsimile Impressment Orders 67
Appendix 4:
    A Colonial Listing of Wages 68
Appendix 5:
    Demographic & Service Information, Command Structure,
    1755-1762, Col. Bagley's Regiments 71
Appendix 6:
    Command Structure, 1755-1762, Col. Bagley's Battalions .. 75
Appendix 7:
    Transcription, Jonathan Bagley Orderly Book, 1758 89

Select Bibliography 103

Index: 109

Illustrations, Maps, and Tables:

Maps:

Map 1. Southern Battle Theater of 1755-1758,
   Jonathan Bagley's Regiment x
Map 2. Northern Battle Theater 1759-1760
   Jonathan Bagley's Regiment 4
Map 3. Areas of Significant Residency at Recruiting, 1756,
   Jonathan Bagley's Regiment 8

Illustrations:

Fig. 1 A depiction of Bagley and part of his regiment at Ft.
   William Henry re-supplying their new fortification, 1756 2
Fig. 2 Stockbridge Mohicans 11
Fig. 3 Auxiliary Corps, Bagley's Regiment 12
Fig. 4 A depiction of Bagley arriving at
   the 1758 rendezvous at Albany, NY 16
Fig. 5 Sailor clothing mixed with uniforms 28
Fig. 6 Great coats and cold weather gear 34
Fig. 7 A depiction of Bagley and unit departing
   for Ticonderoga with flags flying 40
Fig. 8 Regimental flag, New England Pine Tree Flag
   and Country flag, Red Ensign 41
Fig. 9 Issued military gear 42
Fig. 10 Drummers to be in green coats, 1759 43
Fig. 11 Full issue clothing and gear, 1760 44
Fig. 12 Field and Company officer's dress 45
Fig. 13 Capt. Mason in Company officer's dress,
   oil painting Peabody Essex Museum, Salem, MA. ... 46
Fig. 14 Women camp followers 57

Tables:

Range of Age for Soldiers, 1756, Jonathan Bagley's Regiment .. 65
Bagley's Regiment, A Colonial Listing of Wages 68
Per-month 1991 Money Equivalence Bagley's Regiment,
   1755-1760 70

Acknowledgments

When looking back on the character of this research three men of Bagley's Regiment come to the front who in their writings proliferate the feelings of the soldiers of Colonel Jonathan Bagley's Regiment. Lt. Samuel Greenleaf, Centinel Gibson Clough, and Centinel Joseph Nichols seem to pour forth the emotions, true affects, and personalities of these citizen soldiers.

It is primarily through the contemporary writing of diaries, orderly books, letters, and papers that I have attempted to seize the experiences of Bagley's soldiery during this precursor to the American Revolution. Seen and felt from their perspective when serving with the British Red Coats are the building of animosities and the fueling towards an ultimate eruption. Before and in the beginning of this conflict Bagley's men thought of themselves as Freeborn Englishmen with all the rights and privileges bestowed upon them as such. Ultimately, these Yankees of the Bay Colony after seeing and being subjected to the personalities, servitude, and culture of the regulars began to see themselves as another breed of freemen.

While still serving their country these citizen soldiers developed techniques and attitudes of dealing with their new feelings and eventually drew on this a decade later to establish themselves as FREEMEN, FREEHOLDERS, AND CITIZEN SOLDIERS of their own dominion.

In acknowledging assistance in the research of this history two people were instrumental. Fred Anderson, author of *A People's Army* willingly shared his research of the soldiers of Massachusetts. Our phone conversations and the sharing of his research notes led me to fill some voids in my research and pointed the way to other information. The second person, Ms. Kim Frazho, of the Houghton Lake Public Library helped more than any other. She relentlessly searched and acquired through the Public Library the majority of the documents used in this history. Kim not only exhausted the inter-library loan systems but used her own phone to make connections to receive information and opened the doors for visitations of several archives.

Several archives and libraries were exceptionally helpful in assisting my research trips. The professional hospitality was appreciated from the following institutions: American Antiquarian Society, Worcester, MA.; Massachusetts Historical Society, Boston, MA.; Clements Library, Ann Arbor, MI.; Pell Research Center, Ft. Ticonderoga, Ticonderoga, NY.; Amesbury Public Library, Amesbury, MA.; Peabody Essex Museum, Salem, MA.; Williams College Archives, Williamstown, MA.; Bartlett Museum, Amesbury, MA.

I must also thank two individuals for their proofreading. Don Mainprize diligently proofread the rough draft of this history several years ago and showed his expertise in the historical citation format. Maureen Talarico was kind enough to proofread my final draft and encouraged me in the pursuit of publication.

I have not alluded in this history to my private obsession. I am a living historian, as well as professional historian, public school teacher, and college professor. Six years ago when I started research on this history I started a new living history organization, "Colonel Jonathan Bagley's Massachusetts Provincial Regiment." My family and I had been doing living history for ten years but at that time wished to invent our own. This has given me the opportunity to field test my theories and finds. Through the years our group has grown and have prided ourselves in camaraderie, educating the public, and the sharing of research. It is with great pride that I publicly thank all our members past and present in helping with their enthusiasm to encourage me to compile and organize this research.

I must also thank the artist of the drawings within. Joseph Lee, a friend and fellow living historian has used his God-given talents to bring forth my mental images. I am not sure if Joe knows his true potential and talents, but he humbly continues his never-ending dedication to art, which is shown in his many contributions to literature.

I would finally like to thank my family for their help in this history. I thank my mother for giving me my organizational skills, my father for taking us to museums and historic sites when growing up, and my wife Karen for her continued encouragement, love, and being my living history partner.

Dedication of this history goes to my son Brent who has pursued living history with me for his fourteen years. It is when Brent dons his regimental coat, soldier's hat, and sailor's slops and stands in the ranks of Bagley's Regiment that I am proudest. His mother and I are proud of his diligence of study at a young age and his urgency to correct wrong information at sites and museums. We are proud that some of the morals and standards these historic soldiers lived by are imbedded in him.

Thanks Son

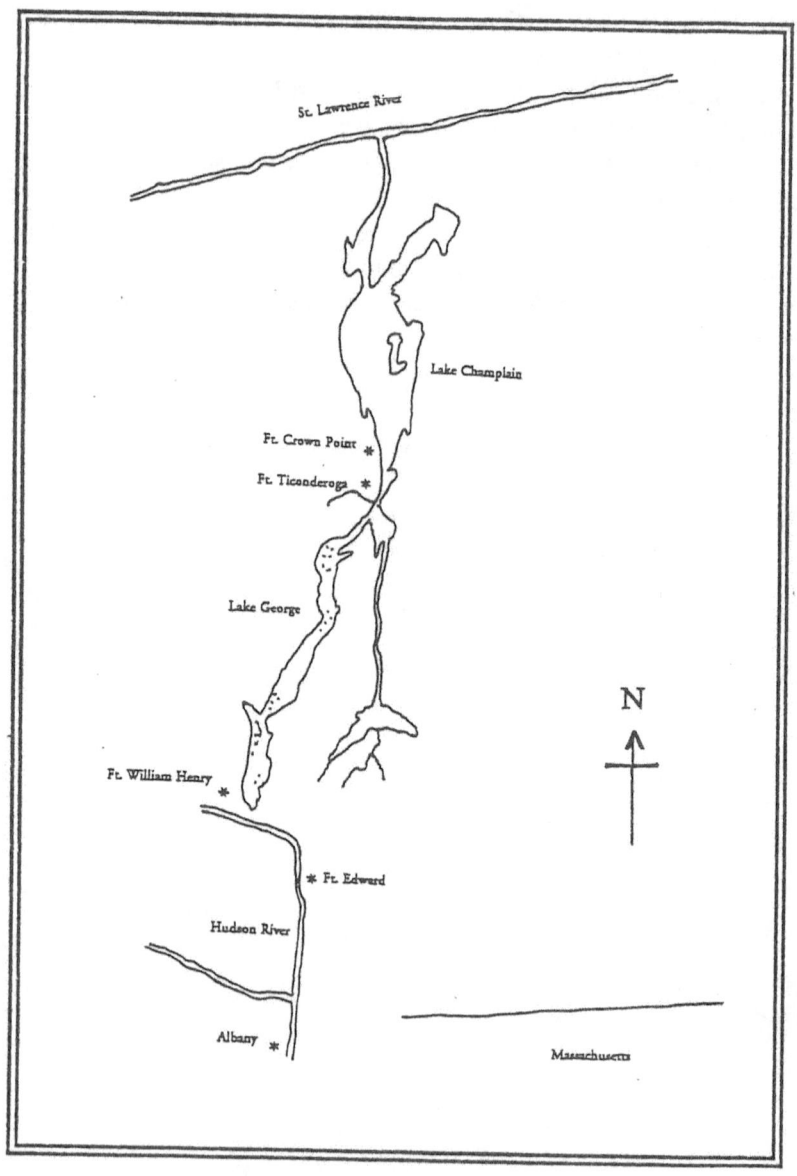

Map 1. **Southern Battle Theater of 1755-1758**
Jonathan Bagley's Regiment
Cartography by Brenton C. Kemmer

Part I:

FREEMEN, FREEHOLDERS, AND CITIZEN SOLDIERS

As it is the essential property of a free government to depend on no other soldiery but its own citizens for its defense; so in all free governments, every freeman and every freeholder should be a soldier.[1]

Lt. Col. Jonathan Bagley's Regiment of the Massachusetts Provincials was part of the all citizen army which launched into the defense of their country against the French Catholics and their Indian allies attempting to expand their feudal empire south and eastward. In 1755, Col. Moses Titcomb, Lt. Col. Bagley and their men headed west from Massachusetts to rendezvous with Gen. William Johnson of New York. General Johnson's all provincial army was given the challenge of forcibly removing the French from their entrenchments that the English called Crown Point and Ticonderoga in northern New York Colony. The army advanced to Lake George where they set up an encampment to prepare for their attack on these forts.

The French simultaneously were sending south a force of regulars, militia, and Indians to attack Johnson's army. The Baron Dieskau, commander of the French forces, surprised one of Johnson's scouting parties and swung his army towards the provincial camp. When the provincials began to retreat back into their lines, panic nearly erupted. The commanders formed their regiments into fortified positions, turning over wagons and boats, and felling trees. Titcomb and Bagley formed their regiment on the right. The provincials decisively held their own against multiple thrusts from the French. This battle ensued all day and in the afternoon the right received a heavy frontal assault

---

[1] *The Exercise for the Militia Of the Province of the Massachusetts-Bay*, Printed and Sold by John Draper & Printers for His Excellency the Captain-General, &c. 1758, Boston, p. 3, Early American Imprints 1639-1800 Supplement, Dr. Clifford K. Shipton editor, Evans Collection #40981, American Antiquarian Society, Worcester, Mass., microprint, 1968.

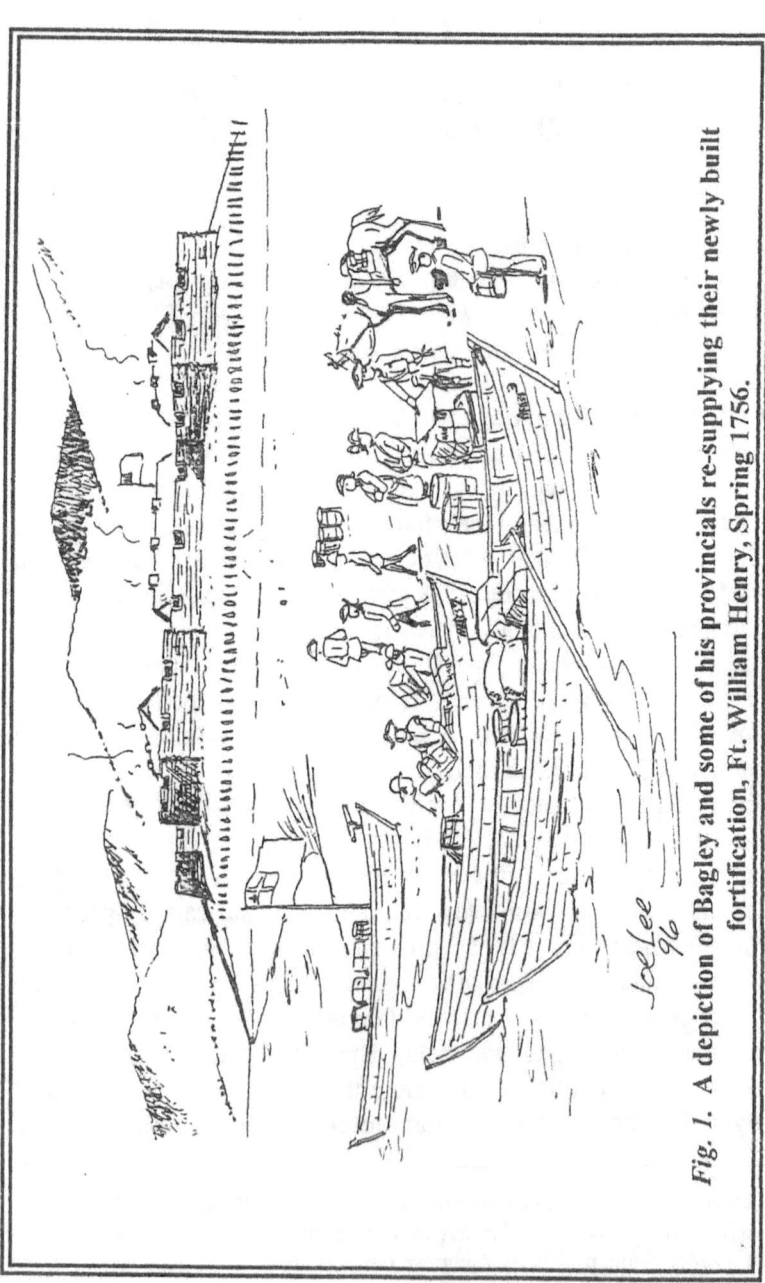

Fig. 1. A depiction of Bagley and some of his provincials re-supplying their newly built fortification, Ft. William Henry, Spring 1756.

from the French regulars. Many of the men fought from behind the trees, as did Col. Titcomb who was shot dead. Lt. Col. Bagley assumed command of the regiment, not letting it falter, but rather successfully repulsed the French regulars. At the end of the battle the provincials were in possession of the field of battle, the French were in retreat back to Carillon (Fort Ticonderoga), and the Baron Dieskau was mortally wounded and held captive by Johnson and his army. Bagley's men fought with great valor and helped win the only English victory in North America in 1755. Of the provincials Dieskau said, "In the morning they fought like good boys, about noon like men, and in the afternoon like devils." [2]

Shortly after the Battle of Lake George, General Johnson ordered a fort to be built near the camp and battle site. This fort was named Fort William Henry. When Gen. Johnson left for the year, Jonathan Bagley, stationed at Fort William Henry, was not only made a colonel to replace Moses Titcomb, but was also made commandant of both Fort William Henry and Fort Edward (see map 1). Many of Bagley's men stayed on at Fort William Henry and were paramount in its construction in 1755 (see fig. 1).

Bagley's regiment returned to this same battle theater in 1756 and 1757 and as before, they functioned as carpenters, boat builders, and garrison troops. They were stationed at both Fort William Henry and Fort Edward. Bagley's regiment was perfectly suited for this assignment because many were civilian carpenters. The vast majority of his men had been recruited from two maritime towns. Many of the men were trained shipwrights. It was only normal for them to take up the ax, adze, saw, and mallet. And build they did! Not only did Bagley's regiment construct most of Fort William Henry, but they were some of the major boat builders for the English army. Evans, Clough, Currier, Flanders, Hacket, Hunt, Lowell, Merrill, Moggaridge, Morrill, Osgood, Stockman, Swett, Webster, Whitcomb, Wingate, and Woodwell were all in Bagley's regiment and back home these names were, or were to become, synonymous with the history of New England boat building.

---

[2] Francis Parkman, *Montcalm and Wolfe* (New York: Atheneum, 1984), 181.

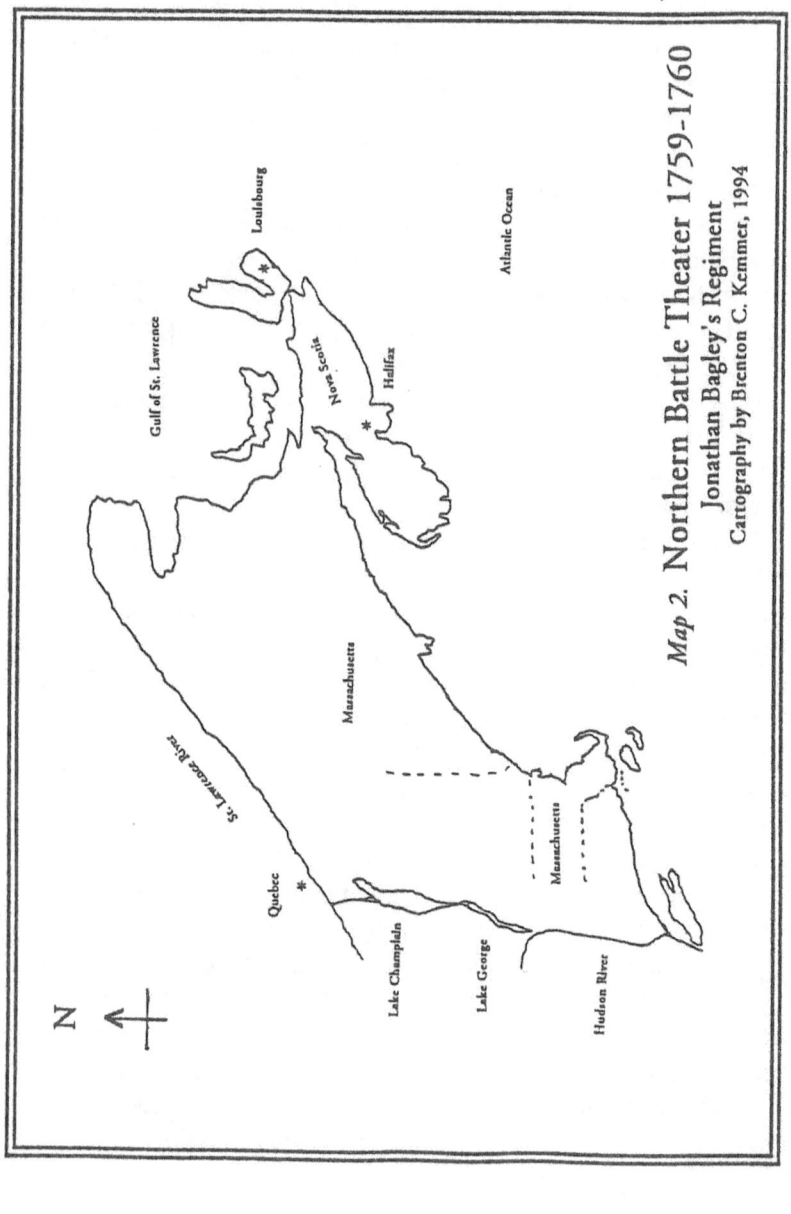

Map 2. Northern Battle Theater 1759-1760
Jonathan Bagley's Regiment
Cartography by Brenton C. Kemmet, 1994

FREEMEN, FREEHOLDERS, AND CITIZEN SOLDIERS 5

The year of 1758 brought Bagley's regiment into the center of a great battle in the area of New York for a second year. They advanced to an encampment near the place where Fort William Henry had stood until the French burned it down in 1757. There, Bagley and his men prepared for an assault on Fort Ticonderoga. This time the army was an amalgamation of regulars and provincial troops. When the flotilla of near 15,000 soldiers took to the waters of Lake George, the Massachusetts regiments were given the place of honor on the right flank with Bagley and Lieutenant Colonel Whitcomb in the lead boat of the third regiment. In the advance at the army's landing near Fort Ticonderoga, Bagley covered the right flank and charged on that flank, helping to successfully push the enemy from this forward position. The next day turned out to be the most devastating of the war; Bagley's regiment was drawn up near the left flank beside the New York regiment. This battle raged unsuccessfully all day with devastating losses to the English who were sent forward without artillery support. Bagley's regiment had 2 officers and 4 centinels (privates) killed, and 11 men were wounded during this engagement.[3]

In the last two years of fighting in North America, the men in Bagley's regiment saw service in the extreme northern campaigns at Fortress Louisbourg in Nova Scotia (see map 2). By this time the English had imported so many regulars that many of the provincials like Bagley's were being used for garrisons, scouting, escort parties, and on support and fatigue details. Holding true to their beliefs, Bagley and his men served in many capacities for the defense of their country and colony. Though not always as obedient as the regulars would have liked it, these men supported their common cause with the enthusiasm of freemen, freeholders, and citizen soldiers.

Many histories have been written about the Seven Years' War and books have been written on selected types of soldiers who fought in this first global conflict. Of these histories, one stands out as historians delve into the soldiery of Massachusetts-Bay. Fred

---

[3] "Journal of Reverend John Cleaveland, June 14, 1758 - October 25, 1758," *Fort Ticonderoga Museum Bulletin*, #10 (1959): 200.

Anderson's *A People's Army* holds the keys to the definitive social-military history of this colony's soldiery.[4]

This volume will enhance historical research of the period. This organizational history of Colonel Jonathan Bagley's regiment, which participated in the Seven Years' War from 1755 through 1760, will not only give a history of Bagley's unit, it will also give an inside look at soldiers' lives. This book will explain the daily lives of Bagley's Massachusetts soldiers, including their religion, illness and medical care, disobedience, diet, wages, clothing, gear, and equipment.

Jonathan Bagley was born on March 23, 1717, in Amesbury, Massachusetts, to Orlando Bagley and Dorothy Harvey Bagley. Orlando was a large land owner, teacher, selectman, and trial justice. Jonathan was the sixth child of twelve in a family of seven boys and five girls. The Bagleys were prominent in the community of Amesbury and for a while Orlando had married more couples than the local minister. Jonathan married Dorothy Wells of Amesbury on December 9, 1736. She was the daughter of the town's minister, Reverend Wells. They had eleven children; seven boys and four girls. Jonathan began his adult career as a husbandman living at the Amesbury Ferry in a house built by Timothy Currier, his uncle. In 1741, he built a fifty-foot-wide wharf between Lowell's and Currier's wharves from the bank to the channel of the Pow Wow River. This was at the junction of the Pow Wow and Merrimac Rivers. Jonathan purchased another house, land, and an adjacent ferry in 1750. By 1750, Jonathan owned several vessels; one was a sloop that he built, captained, and sailed to the West Indies. When his father died, Jonathan inherited nine acres, and for many years he purchased and developed additional lands in Massachusetts, New Hampshire, and Maine. By 1756 Jonathan had

---

[4] Fred Anderson, *A People's Army, Massachusetts Soldiers and Society in the Seven Years' War* (New York: W. W. Norton and Co., 1984); Henry L. Gipson, *The Great War For The Empire, the Victorious Years, 1758-1760* (New York: Alfred A. Knopf, Inc.) vol. 7, 1949; Francis Jennings, *Empire of Fortune* (New York: W. W. Norton and Co., 1988); Brent Kemmer, *The Metamorphosed Soldiers of the French and Indian War* (Bentley, Michigan: Cabin Craft, 1991); Robin May, *Wolfe's Army* (London: Men at Arms, Osprey Publishing, 1974); Parkman; Howard H. Peckham, *The Colonial Wars, 1689-1762* (Chicago: The University of Chicago Press, 1964); Ian K. Steele, *Betrayals, Fort William Henry and the Massacre* (New York: Oxford University Press, 1990).

earned the landed gentry's title of esquire. In 1751, he built a third home in Salisbury Point, next to Amesbury on the Merrimac. In 1761 he purchased Stephen Emery's grist mill. For his service in the Seven Years' War Bagley was granted land in Cumberland County, Maine. In 1768 he and Col. Moses Little settled families on this land. He also became a pioneer of Maine's lumber business, owning his own saw mill and had a lime kiln back home on the Merrimac River. He became so wealthy that between 1759 and 1769 Jonathan paid more taxes than anyone else in the Amesbury East Parish.

Jonathan started his public life in 1740. Elected to the Massachusetts House of Representatives in 1743, he served eleven terms. Jonathan served in many different public offices. His military career started in 1740 as a company clerk. In 1743 Jonathan was promoted to lieutenant of the militia. In 1746 he was a captain of the 5th company of the 5th Massachusetts Regiment under Col. Robert Hale which served at the 1745 assault on Fortress Louisbourg in Nova Scotia. In 1755, at the age of thirty-eight, Bagley served as a lieutenant colonel and then was promoted to colonel. He again was commissioned colonel in 1756-62, 1767-69, 1773, and 1774. At age fifty-seven Jonathan left the army and retired to a lucrative civilian life until his death on December 28, 1780, at age sixty-three.[5]

The soldiers of Bagley's regiment as well as the Massachusetts troops as a whole were exceptionally literate for this period. Despite this fact, many primary documents have been lost or destroyed. In collecting research for a demographic study, muster rolls, victualling records, and other returns are not available for every year of the war. Because of this, I have selected the most complete year of information, 1756. In 1756 Bagley's officers corps consisted of himself as colonel, one lieutenant colonel, one major, twelve captains, nineteen lieutenants, and fourteen ensigns; a total of forty-eight officers. Of

---

[5] Amesbury Public Library Archives, "Bagley Family History," Amesbury Public Library, Amesbury, Massachusetts, Donated by Leonard Johnson, Sept. 1968, p. 24-31; Martha Anderson and Norton Bagley, "Some Descendants of Orlando Bagley of Amesbury, Massachusetts," Genealogical Society of the Church of Jesus Christ of Latter-Day Saints (microfilm, 1973) 1: 5-6, 14-16, 34-36; Fred Anderson, to Brenton C. Kemmer, 1994, Massachusetts Archival Records for Bagley Family, Author's Private Collections, Houghton Lake, Michigan.

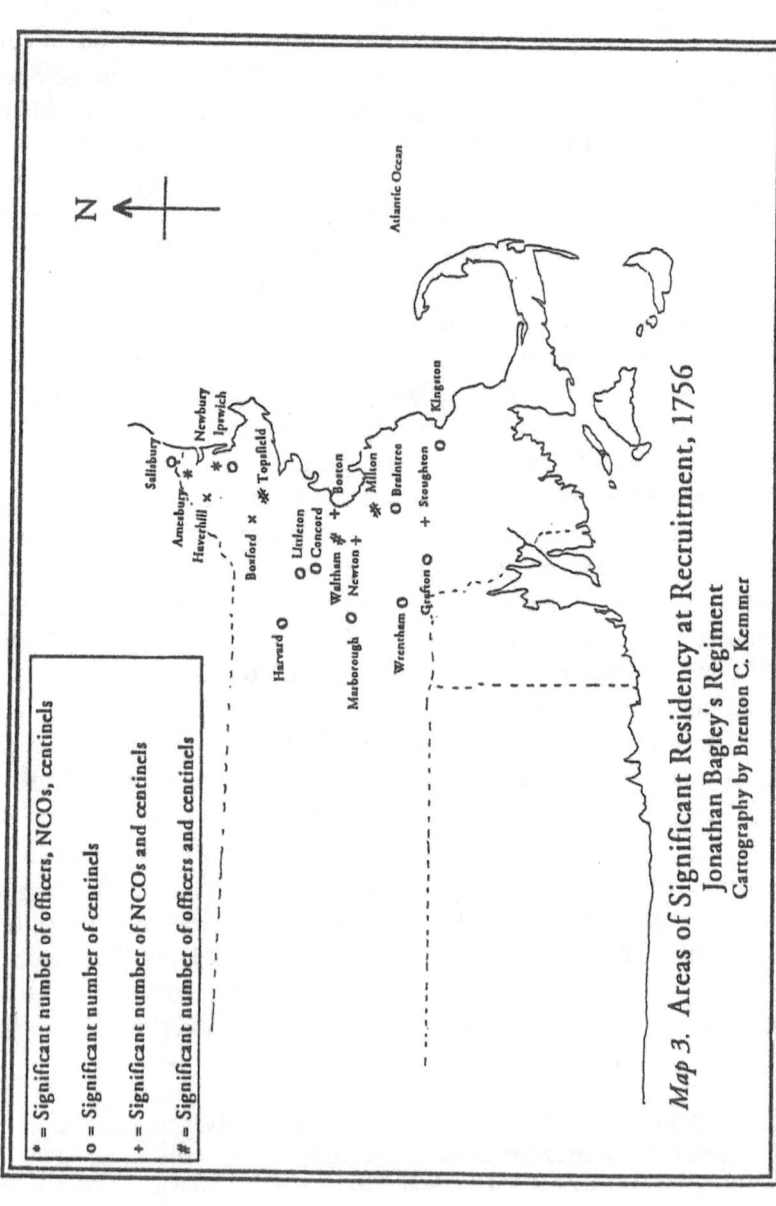

Map 3. Areas of Significant Residency at Recruitment, 1756
Jonathan Bagley's Regiment
Cartography by Brenton C. Kemmer

these officers, 46 percent were recruited from the towns of Amesbury and Newbury, 23 percent from each (see map 3). These towns are two maritime northeastern Massachusetts towns prominent on the Merrimac River. Fifteen percent of Bagley's officers came from towns around Boston. Thirty percent of the officers were recruited from ten miles west of Boston. The other 9 percent were from scattered Massachusetts towns. All forty-eight officers were volunteers.

When looking at the ages of Bagley's officers, the ensigns averaged 26 years, but ranged from 21 to 36. The lieutenants averaged 29 and ranged from 19 to 35. The captains averaged 31, and ranged from 29 to 43. The major was 29, the lieutenant colonel 38, and Colonel Bagley 39. Forty-four percent of Bagley's officers were between 29 and 30 in 1756.

In evaluating the non-commissioned officers' (NCOs) demographics and residencies I found that Bagley had thirty sergeants and forty-four corporals in 1756. All of them enlisted as volunteers except three corporals and one hired sergeant. One sergeant was impressed into service. When looking at the ages of the NCOs, we find many men over 35. Corporals ranged in age from 19 to 53. Corporals averaged 28. Sergeants ranged from 20 to 45, but averaged 30. In looking at the residency of the NCOs, the greatest percentage came from around Newbury and Amesbury. The second largest NCO recruitment area was from towns greater than ten miles west of Boston. This area produced 26 percent of Bagley's NCOs. Eleven percent of the NCOs came from south of Boston. Eight percent came from Boston and eight more from the towns around Boxford, just north of Boston. Ten percent had no residency listed.

Surviving lists show 456 centinels in Bagley's 1756 regiment. These were primarily a volunteer force. Ninety-four percent volunteered, 4 percent were hired, and 2 percent were impressed into service. The average age of Bagley's centinels was 25, but ages ranged from 16 to 55. Forty-three percent of them were from 16 to 20, 36 percent from 21 to 30, 11 percent from 31 to 40, 8 percent from 41 to 50, and 2 percent over 50. One fourteen-year-old drummer appeared on the lists.

The largest number of centinels came from Newbury and Amesbury. Forty-two percent came from this area, of which 22 percent were from Newbury. Twenty-one percent of centinels were recruited from the Boston area. Eighteen percent came from towns south of Boston and 14 percent came from towns between Boston and Amesbury. Three percent came from towns more than ten miles west of Boston. Only two percent of Bagley's men came from another colony and they all were from New Hampshire. Bagley had no men in 1756 from any other country.

The only other possibility would have been that a very minute number of Bagley's centinels were Indians, Blacks, or as one man was listed, Spanish Indian. Stockbridge Indians (Mohicans) or mixed bloods were the probable racial diversities (see fig. 2). In 1754 through 1756 the Bay Colony had raised Stockbridge Indians into a company of their own under a white Massachusetts officer. These Indians received everything given to the other soldiers of the colony. In July of 1756, their company was disbanded and most went into other service under Robert Rogers in his newly forming ranging corps. Some of these Mohicans joined other Massachusetts companies. Capt. Taplin's company of Bagley's regiment in 1756 for instance had at least one Indian in its ranks. Sir William Johnson, English Commissioner of Indian Affairs, ordered allied Indians to wear a red fillet round their heads.[6]

No information exists on Bagley's auxiliary corps. Of the men found, Bagley had 8 drummers, 2 adjutants, 2 armorers and 1 armorer's assistant, 1 chaplain, 11 clerks, 2 commissaries, 1 surgeon and 2 surgeons' mates, 1 quartermaster, and 1 secretary (see fig. 3).[7]

---

[6] Patrick Frazier, *The Mohicans of Stockbridge* (Lincoln, Nebraska: University of Nebraska Press, 1992), 116; *Samuel Greenleaf Accounts 1756-1767*, Pre-Revolutionary Diaries 1635-1774, (Boston: Massachusetts Historical Society), 211, microfilm; William H. Hill, *Old Fort Edward Before 1800* (Privately Printed, Fort Edward, N.Y., by the Author, 1929), 71.

[7] *Massachusetts Officers in the French and Indian Wars, 1748-1763*, The Society of Colonial Wars, ed. Nancy S. Voye (Boston: The New England Historic Genealogical Society, 1975); *Massachusetts Officers and Soldiers in the French and Indian Wars, 1755-1756*, The Society of Colonial Wars, ed. David Gross and David Zarowin (Boston: The New England Historic Genealogical Society, 1985; *Acts and Resolves, Public and Private, of the Province of the Massachusetts-Bay*, 15 (Boston, 1908) 631. This source will be referred to as *A&R* for the duration of these notes; Cleaveland, 234-236.

Fig. 2. Stockbridge Mohicans. Indians and mixed bloods of this tribe are chronicled to have been in the Massachusetts Provincial Regiments, 1755-1760.

Fig. 3. Bagley's Auxiliary Corps consisted of these important individuals and many others; (left to right) Armorer, Chaplain, and Surgeon.

A summary of the demographic and other statistics shows that age played a significant role in correspondence to rank in Bagley's regiment. Bagley was older than his officers, and the average ages decreased as rank decreased. The same was also true looking at centinels, corporals, and sergeants (see Appendix 1). These soldiers from top to bottom were a volunteer army. All of Bagley's officers volunteered for service and ninety-four percent of his NCOs and centinels volunteered.

When examining residency, the largest number of Bagley's men came from Newbury and Amesbury; officers, NCOs, and centinels. The officers' and NCOs' second largest area of residency came from towns more than ten miles west of Boston. With more than forty percent of Bagley's officers and soldiers coming from Newbury and Amesbury, one can imagine the cultural similarities of this unit. This area was one of the few coastal spots that did not rely upon an agrarian subsistence. Consequently, Bagley's regiment would have had a large proportion of artisans and laborers. Many of the men held occupations in woodworking, leather working, metalworking, maritime, or cloth working.[8] Early in the forming of these communities farming, fishing, salt making, pipestave making, building of small vessels, and common trades like blacksmiths, carpenters, potters, and shoemakers were prominent. Each family also raised their own sheep, cattle, poultry and grew a garden. Inter-colony commerce soon developed around shipbuilding. Boatyards, wharves, and ferries lined the banks of the Merrimac River and on the Pow Wow River as far as the falls. As early as 1692, large ships were being built in this area. This area, along the Merrimac, eventually became the premiere shipbuilding area on the Atlantic coast. Consequently, a very large component of Bagley's soldiers were skilled maritime workers ranging from dock laborers to shipwrights and ship masters.

Col. Bagley's centinels had another twenty percent residency in established towns around Boston. Because of this, approximately sixty percent of Bagley's regiment hailed from towns with artisan, labor, and maritime trades. Almost forty percent of Bagley's centinels resided just north or south of Boston or more than ten miles west. The

---

[8] Anderson, 28.

vast majority of these men would have been farmers, husbandmen, or laborers. These areas by this time had run out of new lands for young men or sons who wished to break away and start their own homestead and farm separately from the old existing lands. Consequently, the men were locked into an agricultural labor trading economy. Their only way out meant moving west, which took money, or military service. This brought the second largest amount of enlistment. The pay for a Massachusetts Seven Years' War centinel equaled an artisan's wages and provided an insured steady income for the duration of an enlistment.[9]

---

[9] Anderson, 38.

Part II:
THIS DAY NO RUM

In addition to the attractive salary offered by the army, the Massachusetts government sweetened the pot to enhance recruiting. The government also issued enlistment bounties for the soldiers. It was common, as in 1755, for the Provincial government to pay officers for each man recruited. On April 28, 1755, the Massachusetts government, "voted, that there be allowed for enlisting the several soldiers for the Crown-Point expedition, one shilling and six pence each, to be paid to the captains who shall enlist the same."[10] In 1756 this was raised to three shillings. For further incentive, if a soldier re-enlisted in 1756 he received half pay from December 1756 through the last of March 1757, a sum of about $11 in 1991 money equivalents.[11]

Recruiting was standardized for all the Massachusetts regiments. Bagley would receive his commission as a colonel of a regiment for the colony. With his papers, he would receive blank officers' commissions which he dispersed to men who brought him recruits (see Appendix 2, for facsimile officer's commission). In turn, these officers would promise NCO billets to men who brought them recruits. Bagley also received beating orders. These were written orders giving him permission to actively recruit in the colony and also told the militia commanders to cooperate with his enlistment processes. If toward the end of the recruitment time he had not filled his quota then he could impress out of the militias (see Appendix 3, for facsimile impressment orders).[12]

Many men recruited family members. Bagley himself had two sons and at least four other Bagley family members in the service of the Bay Colony in 1756-57. Looking at 1756 there were 447 family

---

[10] Massachusetts Historical Society, *Journal of the House of Representatives of Massachusetts, 1755*, (Boston: Massachusetts Historical Society, 1956) 30: 294. This source will be referred to as *JHR* for the duration of these notes.

[11] "A Broadside of the Establishment of Wages for the Province of Massachusetts-Bay, In the House of Representatives," February 26, 1756, p. 1-2, Broadside Collections, Clements Library, University of Michigan, Ann Arbor, Michigan.

[12] Anderson, 39-42.

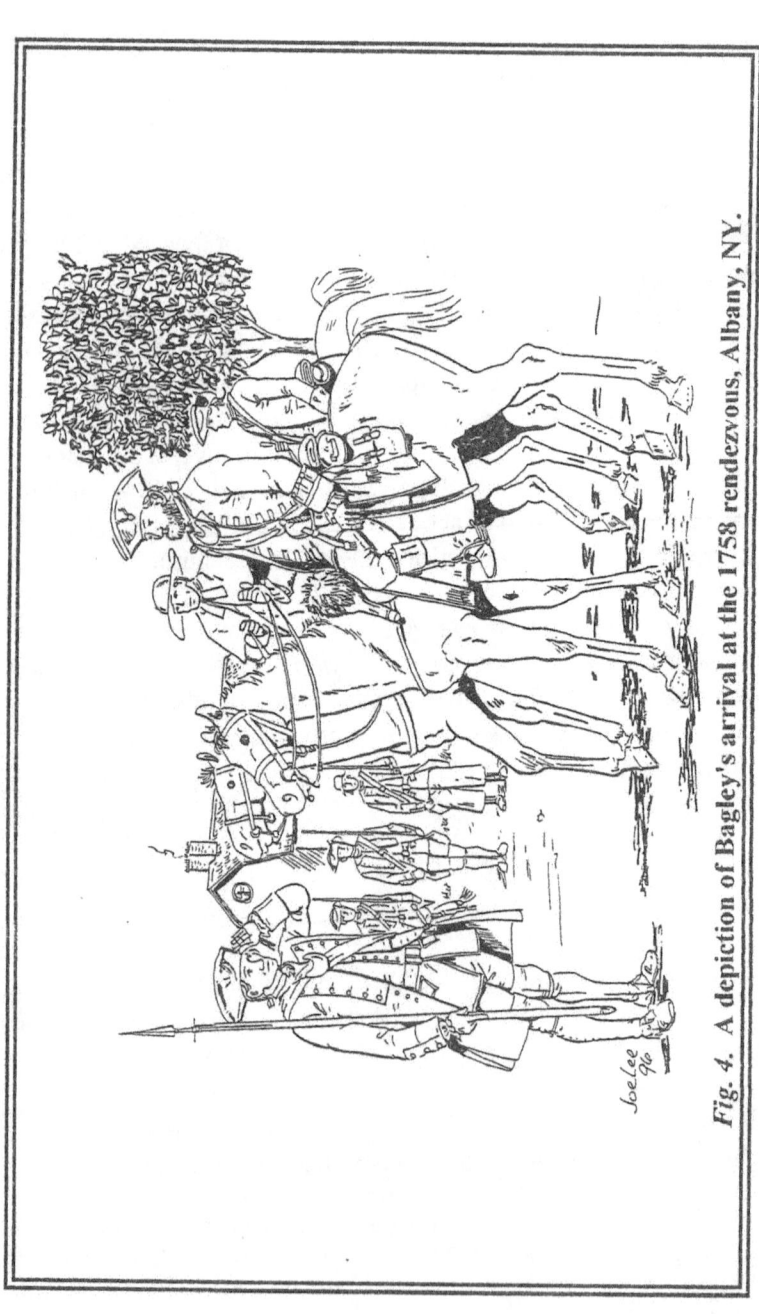

Fig. 4. A depiction of Bagley's arrival at the 1758 rendezvous, Albany, NY.

names listed for Bagley's regiment. Of these, 74 family names appeared more than once. Of the officers, auxiliary corps, NCOs, and drummers, 20 family names showed up. Nine family names repeated five or more times, four being officers' family names. Sixty-eight percent of Bagley's regiment may have been related to another person in the regiment. Of officers ranking lieutenant and higher, there was a 73 percent ratio of relatives. Ensigns only had a 35 percent possibility of having a relative in the unit. Twenty percent of all Bagley's officers may have had a relative as another officer in the regiment. These soldiers, therefore, were connected not only by residency and occupation, but more importantly by the strongest bond of blood.

Once a soldier enlisted in the regiment he received a location to muster. On the designated date, the members of the unit collected at the rendezvous area and, once all met muster, the regiment moved west or north to the annual campaign area (see fig. 4). This occurred annually since enlistment meant only one campaign season, averaging six to twelve months. From 1755 through 1758 Bagley's men marched west to Albany, New York, and then north to Lake George and Lake Champlain. In 1759 and 1760 they traveled east an then north by ship to Nova Scotia.

For the trip the troops received billeting money for subsistence. In 1755 each man got eight shillings per week from their homes to the general rendezvous near the front. If traveling west by land, they had to travel a minimum of fifteen miles a day. The eight shillings equals about $28 a week in 1991 equivalence. Two years later, in 1757, the billeting was only five shillings and eight pence, equaling about $19.[13]

The actual wages received by the men were also linked to their clothing, gear, and food. When looking at the wages, one must keep in mind that these other supplied items enhanced the prospect of soldiering as a whole. Using an annual breakdown of wages per month in 1755 (I have chosen to convert the wages to 1991 equivalencies. For a colonial listing see Appendix 4), Bagley received $896; his lieutenant colonel, $745; major, $634; captain, $336; lieutenant, $224; ensign, $149; chaplain, $448; surgeon, $700; surgeon's mate, $373; adjutant, $149; armorer, $280; armorer's assistant, $140;

---

[13] A&R, 15: 734.

commissary, $224; sergeant, $119; corporal, $104; drummer, $104; and centinel, $93. In 1756 wages stayed about the same. For 1757 wages rose a lot. In that year Bagley was paid $1,200, and his centinels $120. In 1758 the pay for all ranks fell. Bagley's pay dropped to $1,140 and his centinels' pay dropped to $114. In 1759 wages dropped even lower with the exception of Bagley and his adjutant. Bagley then made $1,333 per month and his centinels' pay dropped to $96. In 1760 wages rose partially back to their recorded highs of 1757 when most of the officers had their second best pay year. Other members of the regiment had been paid better two out of the six years. Bagley hit his all time high in 1760, earning $1,416 per month, though his centinels earned only $102 per month. Comparing wages from 1755 through 1760, all members of Bagley's regiment increased in their wages except the surgeon and his mates. Their wages dropped 23 percent during this time. The armorer, his assistant, the commissary, and the quartermaster have incomplete records, precluding a comparison. The chaplain's figures drew a distinction between ministers with established congregations, and those who were not established. Using the figures of 1755-1758 along with 1759-1760, "unestablished" ministers saw only a .08 percent increase for the six-year period. Chaplains who received "established" ministers' wages received a 21 percent increase. The next lowest wage increase for the six years was for sergeants. They only earned a 2 percent increase. The third lowest increase was for corporals and drummers. Their increase was only 4 percent. The bulk of the regiment, the centinels, received an 8 percent wage increase. Next came the officers. These men saw between a 16 and 37 percent increase. The major had the lowest, with a 16 percent increase. Next, with a 20 percent increase came the lieutenants and Bagley's lieutenant colonel. Ensigns received 24 percent more wages. The two types of officers doing the most work were the adjutant and the captains. The adjutant was a secretary in charge of all the paperwork for the entire regiment. The captains had direct control over the companies of Bagley's regiment and served as the link between him and his men. The government must have seen these vital links as well because they received a 34 percent increase over the six years. Bagley himself topped all increases and from 1755-1760 received a 37 percent increase in his wages.[14]

These figures mean that Bagley's centinels earned the 1991 equivalent income in 1760 of $1,224 a year. We find it hard to imagine earning less than $2,000 a year, but for the 1750's this was about the average wage. Bagley earned the equivalent of $16,992. These dollar equivalents show one of the drastic differences between the colonel and his men. Bagley made almost thirteen times more money than his centinels. This created visual differences in the daily military environment. If these men were your neighbors, would you consider them your peers, given this example of inequality?

The second area of payment for the soldiery of Massachusetts-Bay was their food. *The Journals of the House of Representatives* in 1755 recorded that each man was issued 1 pound (16 ounces) of bread, 1 pound of pork, 1 pound of flour, 1/2 pint of peas or beans, 1 pint of Indian meal, 1 pint of molasses, 4 ounces of butter, 2 ounces of ginger, and 1 gill (4 ounces) of rum per day, and also 1 pound of sugar per week. In 1756 each man was issued 14 ounces of bread, 14 ounces of pork, 1 pound of flour, 1/2 pint of peas or beans, 1 pint of Indian meal, 1 pint of molasses, 4 ounces of butter, 2 ounces of ginger, 1 gill of rum per day, and 1/2 a pound of sugar per week.

These two years show the beginnings of variability in rations for the Massachusetts soldiers. Were these rations enough to support a soldier? Using 1991 statistics from the United States Department of Agriculture one can compare caloric intake and evaluate the soldiers' conditions. One pound of bread equals 1,190 calories, 42 grams of protein, 16 grams of fat, and 0 cholesterol. One pound of pork (salted) equals 1,093 calories, 95 grams of protein, 74 grams of fat, and 27 milligrams of cholesterol. One pound of wheat flour equals 420 calories, 12 grams of protein, 1 gram of fat, and 0 cholesterol. One half pint of peas equals 65 calories, 5 grams of protein, and 0 fat or

---

[14] John J. McCusker, *How Much is that in Real Money? A Historical Price Index for Use as a Deflater of Money Values in the Economy of the United States* (Worcester, Massachusetts: American Antiquarian Society, 1992); John J. McCusker, *Money and Exchange in Europe and America, 1600-1775* (Chapel Hill, The University of North Carolina Press, 1978) 141; *A&R*, 501, 669, 686-87; *Ibid.*, 16: 307-09; *JHR*, 30: 285; *Ibid.*, 32 part 1: 62; *Ibid.*, 35: 335.

cholesterol. One half pint of beans equals 170 calories, 10 grams of protein, 1 gram of fat, and 0 cholesterol. One pint of Indian meal (corn meal) equals 435 calories, 20 grams of protein, 5 grams of fat, and 0 cholesterol. One pint of molasses equals 384 calories, 1,360 grams of protein, and 0 fat, and cholesterol. Two ounces of ginger equals 30 calories, 0 grams of protein, 0 grams of fat, and 0 cholesterol. Four ounces of butter equals 810 calories, 1 gram of protein, 92 grams of fat, and 247 milligrams of cholesterol. Two and one quarter ounces of sugar (1/7 of the weekly ration) equals 234 calories and 0 protein, fat, or cholesterol. One gill of rum equals 350 calories and 0 protein, fat, or cholesterol.

In 1756 the bread allowance dropped to 14 ounces, a drop of 149 calories, 5 grams of protein, and 2 grams of fat. The pork ration dropped to 14 ounces also, dropping 136 calories, 11 grams of protein, 9 grams of fat, and 3 milligrams of cholesterol. The sugar ration was cut in half, dropping 117 calories per day.

The 1755 expected daily rations equaled 5,181 calories and 189 grams of fat. Bagley's centinels averaged 25 years of age. According to the United States Department of Agriculture (U.S.D.A.) men ranging in age from 23 to 50 should have a daily caloric intake of 2,700. According to the 1755 rations the soldiers were taking in about 48 percent more calories than needed for their age. With the reductions of 1756, the men still received 43 percent more than they needed.[15] One must keep in mind two things when evaluating caloric intake for soldiers. First, these are speculative issues of food rations that, in fact, were rarely issued or even issued in the quantities the government hoped for. Second, these soldiers exerted a much higher level of energy from drill and work or fatigue parties.

Looking further into the issue of what the men actually saw in rations I find that substitutions were common. In August 1755 Abijah Willard recorded beer substituted for rum.[16] In August of 1756

---

[15] United States Department of Agriculture, Human Nutrition Information Service, "Nutritive Values of Foods," by Susan E. Gebhardt and Ruth H. Matthews, *Home and Garden Bulletin*, #72, (Washington DC: Superintendent of Documents, U.S. Government Printing Office, June, 1991).

[16] "Journal of Abijah Willard of Lancaster, Massachusetts," *New Brunswick Historical Society, Collections*, ed. J. C. Webster, 13: 41.

Samuel Greenleaf, one of Bagley's lieutenants, wrote, "a party of wagons came up from Albany and brought us up 32 squash and 550 (pounds) beans. We had a very good dinner of pork and squash and green beans."[17] Bagley recorded in his orderly book on August 22, 1758, "every man has daily a proportion of roots and greens and that each of them receive daily 1 gill of vinegar from the commissary which the men are to pay for."[18] Not only were the men of Bagley's unit getting some vegetables and vinegar to serve as an alcohol substitute but they were expected to pay for it. On September 14, Bagley also stated that the commissary was to deliver fish for rations.[19] In 1759 a frequent substitute, not liked by the men, was spruce beer, a distilled liquid from spruce boughs boiled in water with molasses and allowed to ferment for a week or so. This substituted for the daily rum ration. "Spruce beer is to be brewed for the health and convenience of the troops which will be served at prime cost; 5 pints of molasses will be put into every barrel of spruce beer. Each gallon will cost near three coppers."[20]

Other supplements came from the soldiers themselves. One could get more or different foods by catching it or buying it. When the soldiers got some free time away from their daily duties, many would hunt or fish. "The deer continue plenty, they dayly bring into camp numbers. Col. Whitcomb this day got seven."[21] Many hunted in large groups as well. Greenleaf in 1756 cited that, "a party of about 200 went out a hunting after deer."[22] Caleb Rea, Bagley's regimental surgeon, enjoyed fishing. "I took another turn on ye lake fishing. The lake affords plenty of fish called Oswego bass, also perch, roach,

---

[17] Greenleaf, 73.

[18] Brenton C. Kemmer, "A Transcription of the Jonathan Bagley Orderly Book, 1758 from the Manuscript in the American Antiquarian Society of Worcester, Massachusetts, 1994," p. 3, Author's Private Collections, Houghton Lake, Michigan.

[19] *Ibid.*, 14.

[20] Hugh Hastings, ed. *Orderly Book and Journal of Hawks* (Syracuse, NY: Society of Colonial Wars, 1901), 3.

[21] F. M. Ray, ed., *The Journal of Dr. Caleb Rea* (Salem: Privately Printed, 1881), 200.

[22] Greenleaf, November 5, 1756.

trouts etc., but ye bass is ye biggest and counted ye best."[23] In September of 1758 Joseph Nichols of Bagley's regiment said, "I was able to go a fishing at the brook, caught me a comfortable mess which I ate for my dinner."[24]

Purchasing additional food was done through the colonial sutlers, or camp stores set up in either tents or huts at the encampments and forts. John Noyes of Bagley's unit in 1758 listed several different items he purchased in camp. Some of the foods were sugar, chocolate, raisins and cheese. Noyes, like many of the soldiers, craved liquor and from June 25, through October 23, he purchased seven pints of alcoholic beverages including wine and snakeroot, but mostly rum.[25] Amos Richardson and Capt. William Sweats on the 1758 campaign to Fort Ticonderoga also purchased milk, and Richardson bought apples, five pence each.[26] William Henshaw actually recorded some prices he paid for tea, sugar, chocolate, and milk in 1759. Tea sold for 8 shillings a pound, sugar 2 pounds for 6 shillings 3 pence, chocolate 3 shillings 6 pence, and milk 2 quarts for 1 shilling and 8 pence. To give an idea of prices, a half gallon of milk cost the equivalent of $4.44 in 1991 money. Henshaw's money bought about 1/3 less than ours does today.[27] Enoch Poor of Bagley's regiment also recorded some items in his diary, "beer is a copper a quart, sugar 8 shillings, snakeroot 6 coppers a gill, rum 6 coppers a gill, cider 8 coppers a quart.[28] The sutlers were out for a profit. They charged exorbitant prices on this warfare frontier. Other foods and drink supplemented were eggs, fowl,

---

[23] Rea, 34.

[24] Joseph Nichols Diary (Henry E. Huntington Library, San Marino, California) MS. HM89, 58, microfilm.

[25] *Journal of John Noyes of Newbury* (Salem: Essex Institute, Historical Collections) vol. 45 (1909) 73-76.

[26] "Amos Richardson's Journal, 1758," *The Bulletin of the Fort Ticonderoga Museum,* vol. 12 (1968): 288-290; Paul O. Blanchette, ed. "Captain William Sweat's Personal Diary of the Expedition Against Ticonderoga, May 2 - November 7, 1758," Essex Institute, Historical Collections 93 (1957) 40, 48.

[27] Hill, 180.

[28] Fred Anderson, to Brenton C. Kemmer, 1994, notes on Enoch Poor Diary 1759, Author's Private Collections, Houghton Lake, Michigan.

strawberries, potatoes, and cider.[29] Joseph Nichols summed it up nicely in 1758: "Our sutlers are fell much in the price of their stores—rum that a few days was sold for one half a dollar for a quart is sold for half the money and much of their stores they gave away. It is justly come upon them for their contortion for they have very much imposed upon our people in this campaign."[30]

The rations along with the examples of supplementals, all paint a rosy picture, but in reality things were far different. Col. Timothy Ruggles writing to Gen. William Johnson in 1755 stated that at Fort Edward and Lake George (where Bagley was) bread could not be sent fast enough.[31] In 1756, Colonel Bagley while commanding officer at Fort William Henry, had his secretary Henry Liddel list the provisions belonging to the province of Massachusetts-Bay in stores at his fort. They were, 3 barrels of rum (approximately 60 gallons each), 11 barrels of molasses (approximately 9 gallons each), 3 barrels of flour (200 lbs. each), 5 barrels of ginger (200 lbs. each), 18 barrels of meal (200 lbs. each), 1 barrel of sugar (200 lbs.), 403 barrels of pork (215 lbs. each), 14 barrels of beef (215 lbs. each), 19 barrels of peas (531 lbs. each), 69,045 loaves of bread (1 lb. each), and 57,100 loaves of bread (1/2 lb. each).[32] With Bagley having a garrison of 206 and using Liddel's provision return there was enough bread for a year, meat for 255 days, peas for 100 days, ginger for 40 days, rum for 21 days, meal for 18 days, sugar for 14 days, and molasses for only 4 days. This is so if he issued the government's quantities of daily rations. This means without re-supply in less than one month the calorie intake would drop to 2,565 a day. This is 5 percent below U.S.D.A. recommendations.[33] This must have been anticipated as Samuel

---

[29] "Diary of Nathaniel Knap," *Society of Colonial Wars* (Boston: Society of Colonial Wars, 1895) 5, 11; Willard, 26.

[30] Nichols, 87.

[31] Hill, 91.

[32] Henry Liddel, "A List of Provisions Belonging to the Province of Massachusetts-Bay at Fort William Henry, 1756 Under the Command of Col. Jonathan Bagley," LO 2040 MS. Collections, Henry E. Huntington Library, San Marino, California; Mary C. Hallatt and Lynn M. Lipa, *The King's Bread* (Youngstown, NY: Old Fort Niagara Association, Inc., 1986) 13.

[33] Steele, 62; United States Department of Agriculture.

Greenleaf stated on September 8, three weeks earlier, "This day NO RUM."[34] Bagley evidently started rationing his stores.

Joseph Nichols talked a lot about the deficiencies in Bagley's units' rations in 1758. On August 7, the well men's allowance was butter, rice, and pork (2,227 calories, or 18% deficiency intake). On August 10, pork rations were cut in half. On August 18, Nichols said that four days' ration would only last three. Again on August 26, the men received only pork, rice, and butter. Finally, on September 3, the men in Bagley's unit got some relief. Apples, green lettuce, cucumbers, watermelons, string beans, carrots, cabbage, turnips, and squash arrived at camp. This was short-lived because on September 7, they were only issued pork, flour, and butter in small proportions (19% deficiency). On September 15, things were really desperate. The men decided that three of the six mess mates would go without food one day out of every four. This continual deficiency for more than two months physically and mentally changed the soldiery of Bagley's regiment. I must rely on Joseph Nichols again to summarize the toll this took on Bagley's men.

> *Our army very much uneasy with their manner of living. Our allowance at present is only flour and pork. No rum nor sugar to be had in our regiment for our sutlers are not yet come and we labor under a great disadvantage which other regiments are favored with. The spirit of men seem to fail. I doubt we are loosing our courage that in years past we had the credit of. It is a common saying that money makes the man to go, and make no doubt if in case our natures was refreshed with diet agreeable to what we are used to our strength and courage would come to us like an armed man. It would be understood in a natural course.*[35]

---

[34] Greenleaf, 85.
[35] Nichols, 26-27, 38, 41, 47, 59, 61, 66.

Once in a while Bagley would pull through, as on September 25, 1760. This day he gave his regiment a barrel of rum.[36] Bagley needed to do things like this for his men. He not only needed their respect to lead them into battle or to work diligently for him, but he also needed to appease their probable disgust at his own culinary fare compared to theirs. It was common that officers would receive multiple rations to accommodate their rank, entertain other officers, and feed their servants. In the Bay Colony officers received allowances for their table. Jonathan Bagley was no exception.

In 1755, Bagley had not received his table allowance as he had expected and, in April 1756, he petitioned the Massachusetts House of Representatives for his allowance. They ordered the treasury to pay him 33 pounds, 15 shillings, for his table and other expenses from February 1755 through March 1756.[37] When converted into 1991 equivalence he received $3,375. What an extreme difference compared to his men! He must have looked like royalty to his hometown freeholders.

General Seth Pomeroy in his journal said he stopped twice to eat with General William Johnson on their way north in 1755. The first time they ate ham, baked bread, cheese, lemon punch, and wine. The second meal they ate cold venison, lemon punch and wine.[38] In 1756 and other years, the House of Representatives ordered the Committee of War to supply stores they judged convenient for field officers, chaplains, and surgeons.[39] In 1758 Bagley's chaplain, John Cleaveland, records in his diary a meal with Gen. Abercromby, "soup first, boiled beef, roast beef, boiled fish, fried fish all fresh sodden venison and new potatoes, a plumb pudding, apple pie and cheese."[40] These men would have superior pay, extreme amounts of money to

---

[36] "Diary Kept at Louisbourg, 1759-1760, by Jonathan Procter of Danvers," (Salem: Essex Institute, Historical Collections) 70 (1934) 48.

[37] *A&R*, 15: 504.

[38] Louis Effingham de Forest, ed., *The Journal and Papers of Seth Pomeroy, Sometime General in the Colonial Service* (New Haven, Connecticut, 1926) 110-111.

[39] *A&R*, 328.

[40] Cleaveland, 219.

furnish their fine frontier tables with, and special stores of goods set up for them.

In 1758, Joseph Nichols witnessed and chronicled the activities of the servants of the Massachusetts officers. "This morning observed Colonel William's waiter pass by me carrying squash and carrots. Colonel Bagley's waiter caught several dozen pigeons with a net. I could not but think of the Israelites for the fruits of Egypt."[41] What a sight this must have been to behold, officers dining at tables and chairs, entertaining other officers with their servants preparing their meals!

---

[41] Nichols, 41.

Part III:
AN APPEARANCE OF UNIFORMITY

The third form of pay for the Massachusetts men was clothing and gear. Francis Parkman, in *Montcalm and Wolfe*, states that at the Battle of Lake George one of the corps was dressed in a blue, red faced uniform.[42] In August 1755, a letter in the Sterling papers cites a rush order for, "extra shirts, shoes, stockings, and breeches for the men–a thousand pair of breeches, red in color and made of some good strong woolen stuff."[43] Many orders from the House of Representatives call for clothing and gear for the men of the colony. Some of these call for warm clothing, blankets, and packs.[44]

General Pomeroy listed the following items from his soldiers that were lost at the Battle of Lake George: 5 hatchets, 1 haversack, 12 blankets, 11 trump lines, 1 knife, 2 jackets, 2 waistcoats, 2 hats, 2 caps, and 2 pair of shoes.[45] Capt. Dwight wrote that each man in his company was issued a blanket, knapsack, hatchet, powder, bullets, bullet bags, worms and wires, and fire kettles for the company.[46]

These documents reveal that the centinels and NCOs of Massachusetts regiments wore military clothing at the war's beginning; therefore, uniforming had started. All of the Massachusetts troops received the listed gear to mix with their civilian clothes sometime in 1755.

Uniforms and civilian clothing were essentially the same in the eighteenth century. A shirt, the basic garment, was not only the shirt but also served as undershirt and night shirt as well. These were usually linen or coarse muslin, but wealthier persons also had cotton.

---

[42] Parkman, 171.

[43] John A. Schutz, *William Shirley, King's Governor of Massachusetts* (Chapel Hill: The University of North Carolina Press, 1961) 211.

[44] A&R, 386; JHR, 34 part 1: 170; Pomeroy, 112.

[45] Pomeroy, 143-44.

[46] "The Journal of Capt. Nathaniel Dwight of Belchertown, Massachusetts, During the Crown Point Expedition, 1755," (New York: New York Genealogical and Biographical Record) 33 (1902) 5.

Fig. 5. Bagley's soldiers commonly mixed civilian clothing with issued items. Here are maritime workers in Bagley's Regiment wearing civilian sailor clothing like slops with regimental issued clothing.

Most shirts were bleached or non-bleached white to off-white in color, but some came checked or striped. Soldiers were usually issued several shirts, some white and some checked. Around the neck, a man wore a cravat or cloth to close and cover the shirt, that showed outside the other garments. Some men wore "stocks," a band of fabric that fastened in the back of the neck with ties or buckles. The more affluent also wore a "jabot," which was a laced or linen-layered fabric worn to cover the collar and front of the shirt. Fashionable shirts had lace around the cuff and neck opening.

Around the legs, a soldier wore long stockings to the knee fastened by garters. Pants of the day usually didn't cover the bottom half of the leg. The breeches usually had a button-fly front called a French fly. They were cut full and quite baggy in the seat. Breeches or britches were made of canvas, linen, wool, or leather. Many of Bagley's soldiers would have been wearing "slops" instead of breeches. These were sailor's pants. They were cut like breeches but the leg was left open at the knee. This gave sailors easier movement onboard ships and docks. The length varied from knee length to the ankles. Many were made of sail cloth (linen canvas) (see fig. 5).

Many soldiers covered their legs for protection on the frontier. One method involved wrapping wool or leather around the leg and tying it as the Indians did. These were called leggings. The second involved wearing gaiters, which were canvas or leather tubes that buttoned up the outside of the leg and tied or strapped just below the knee. It was common for the soldiers to be issued canvas gaiters.

Over the shirt the Massachusetts soldiers usually wore a waistcoat (wastecoat, wescut, weskit). It looked like a modern vest but came down to the middle of the thigh. In colonial days a man usually would not walk around in public in just his shirt. Some working men and frontiersmen wore a hunting or working man's frock or smock. This was a loose-fitting, heavy linen shirt that a soldier wore over his regular shirt. This was cooler and cheaper to make. Many military units were issued these work smocks to protect the uniform during work details.

Over the waistcoat the soldier wore a coat, sleeved and buttoned up the front. These coats could have collars or not, and many hung to the mid thigh or longer and covered the waistcoat, which was usually made of linen or wool. The fabrics and colors of the coat and waistcoat did not necessarily match. Massachusetts military coats, or regimentals, as they were called, were made of wool, usually blue and often lapelled and cuffed in another color such as red, blue or green.

The most common soldier's shoe was a round-toed leather shoe with a low heel and a stitched, welted sole. The shoe fastened at the vamp by a buckle, but sometimes with a ribbon or lacing. Some men also bought or fashioned Indian shoes (moccasins) and many officers wore boots resembling riding boots of today.

The soldier's hat was a tricorn; a round hat that was laced up on three sides to form three corners. Tricorns were made of felt made from animal fur, the finest of which were made from beaver. These soldier's hats were black and were edged with white wool tape called ferreting. Stitched under the looping or tie of the front left side of the hat was worn a cockade of black ribbon held on by a button that matched those on the uniform. Other popular styles for Massachusetts soldiers were round felt hats with the brim left flat, felt hats laced up on only one or two sides, and cloth caps made of multiple rounded triangular sections sewn together. The spot where the points came together formed the top, and the widest portion formed the bottom. The bottom folded into a cuff similar to the way we roll a stocking cap. Caps made of cotton, linen, or wool were common with working men (see fig. 1-12).[47]

---

[47] Linda Baumgarten, *Eighteenth Century Clothing at Williamsburg* (Williamburg, Virginia: The Colonial Williamsburg Foundation, 1988); Peter F. Copeland, *Working Dress in Colonial and Revolutionary America* (Westport, CT: Greenwood Press, 1977); Willet and Phillis Cunnington, *Handbook of English Costume in the Eighteenth Century* (Boston: Plays, Inc., 1972); Gerry Embleton and Phillip Haythornthwaite, "The British Infantry of the Seven Years' War" *Military History Illustrated, Past and Present* #36, May 1991, p. 22-34; Ellen Gehret, *Rural Pennsylvania Clothing* (York, Pennsylvania: George Shumway Publisher, 1976); Beth Gilgun, *Tidings From the 18th Century* (Texarkana, Texas: Rebel Publishing Co., Inc., 1993); Elisabeth McClellan, *Historic Dress in America 1607-1800* (Salem, New Hampshire: Ayer Company Publishers, Inc., 1969); Aileen Ribeiro, *A Visual History of Costume, The Eighteenth Century* (New York: Drama Book Publishers, 1983); Merideth Wright, *Everyday Dress of Rural Americans* (New York: Dover Publications, Inc., 1992).

FREEMEN, FREEHOLDERS, AND CITIZEN SOLDIERS   31

Arms were also important to these soldiers. The *Acts and Resolves* of the colony stated that a man would be issued a musket unless he could furnish his own, in which case he was paid a $4 bounty. Mr. Bollan, evidently an agent for the Bay Colony, was ordered by the court in January of 1755 to purchase 2,500 firearms with bayonets and slings. They specifically ordered him to make sure the firearms were four inches longer than the example he had sent them. Bollan's order included 1,500 barrels of powder and 20,000 flints. In June another 1,000 stands of arms were ordered (muskets with bayonets). By September the colony needed more muskets and issued orders to impress arms with any soldiers that were impressed.[48] By the specifics of a four-inch longer musket, they were probably ordering the 46-inch-barreled "Brown Bess" muskets.[49] If 7,000 Massachusetts men fought in 1755 then at least half carried an issued musket. The others carried a wide range of pieces, mostly smooth-bored hunting or fowling guns. Very few rifles were used during the 1750's. Some of the guns were very nice, some were old reliable hunting guns, and some were relics from one of the previous wars in the century.

Tents were the most common form of housing for the Massachusetts soldier. The standard soldier's wedge tent, six by seven feet wide and six feet high, was made of strong linen-canvas, and housed six centinels. Sergeants' wedge tents, nine by nine, and seven and a half feet high, would house two sergeants. It was common for the soldiers to cut bark to place in their tents to lie on. Provincial troops used wall tents as shown in a woodcut of the encampment of the Battle of Lake George made in 1755. Officers were issued marquees and wall tents, varying in size from about ten by twelve feet and larger. Some officers had several marquees and wall tents for different purposes such as bed chamber, office, and dining.[50] In 1756

---

[48] *A&R*, 15: 264, 266, 304, 352, 387.

[49] Anthony D. Darling, *Red Coat and Brown Bess* (Alexandria Bay, NY: Museum Restoration Service, 1970) 15-25.

[50] Bagley, Aug. 25, 1758 (see Appendix 7); Jerry Olson, to Brenton C. Kemmer, 1991, Facsimile Reproduction of Lewis Lockee, An Essay on Castramentation, Original Printed in London by the Author, 1778, p. 2-4, Author's Private Collections, Houghton Lake, Michigan; Andy Gallup, "Research Reveals Measurements Most Interesting," <u>Journal of the Forces of Montcalm and Wolfe</u>

the men did not have to rely just on tentage. Samuel Greenleaf of Bagley's unit stated, "our men all at work to build themselves houses or huts."[51]

Flags commonly flew in front of the tent of the field officers of Massachusetts camps. Both Willard and Pomeroy mention field officers' colours (flags). Pomeroy says that on September 4, 1755, Colonel Gilbert forgot his flag when he left for Fort Edward. Gilbert, very upset, said he would rather lose his arm. In Willard's journal Colonel Winslow of Massachusetts hoisted his flag in rejoicing. But a month later Colonel Monkton, a regular English officer, wouldn't allow Winslow to carry his regimental colours. Bagley's regiment had colours as well. In 1758 Col. Bagley had his colours posted in his boat in the advancing flotilla heading for Ticonderoga.[52]

As it was with pay and rations, officers had it better in clothing and gear as well. They usually could afford to purchase their clothes. In June Pomeroy left some of his belongings in Albany on his way to the front lines. "In a small trunk I left four or five shirts and necks, some caps, two or three white handkerchiefs, a little bag of gold, my best clothes, coat, jacket and britches, my best wig, best hat, boots and saddle bags."[53] Another officer, Col. Ephraim Williams, killed on the morning of the Battle of Lake George, left an extensive inventory of his belongings at this frontier encampment. The inventory included striped trousers, spotted vest, wig, comb and box, bearskin coat, yellow broadcloth coat, 5 checked shirts and 2 white linen shirts, 2 worsted caps, 2 linen caps, 2 pr. leather stockings (leggings), 2 pr. yarn stockings, 2 pr. worsted stockings, 1 pr. linen stockings, handkerchiefs, beaded belt, leather breeches, black breeches, 2 sets of knee and shoe buckles, towels, sword belt, an assortment of books

---

6 # 4 (Oct. 1993): 16; Arthur L. Perry, <u>Origins in Williamstown</u> (New York: Charles Scribner's Sons, 1894), 343; Williams College Archives, Williamstown, Mass., Fisher Howe Collection, Box 1, F1, p. 2-6, "Battle of Lake George, Prospective Plan of the Battle of Lake George by Samuel Blodget, Engraved by Thomas Johnston, Boston, Sept. 8, 1755; Williams College Archives, re-engraved by Thomas Jeffreys, London, Feb. 2, 1756.

[51] Greenleaf, October 18, 1756.
[52] Pomeroy, 121-22; Nichols, 12; Willard, 29, 39.
[53] Pomeroy, 100-01.

FREEMEN, FREEHOLDERS, AND CITIZEN SOLDIERS 33

such as Roman history, Cato's letters, Bland's *Military Discipline*, *The Independent Whig*, a Psalm book, Testament, and memorandum book. He also left a pen knife, silk purse, and Japanned snuff box.[54] The field officers had most of the luxuries of home. They lived like kings compared to their men, but still commanded their respect.

To haul these items, the Massachusetts regiments employed the teamsters and truckers of the time. They tried to acquire enough wagons and carts to move all the supplies, rations, gear, and tentage. This was a never-ending project. In 1759 a Massachusetts major recorded that every 500 provincials were assigned five wagons and one for staff officers.[55] Because of the terrain of the Lake George-Lake Champlain corridor, water travel was easier. Another thing the army of the 1750's had going for it was trained shipbuilders and sailors, many from Jonathan Bagley's regiment. Several types of boats were used by Massachusetts soldiers. One was a whaleboat – a double-ended boat with a round bottom. Dimensions ranged from 24 to 34 feet. The more common boat for movement of military essentials was the bateau, a double-ended boat with a flat bottom. These bateaux varied in size, depending on the boat's construction and purpose. Bagley's surgeon chronicles at Fort Edward in October of 1758, "our Regiment ordered to serve here as bateauxmen." [56] These not only carried the soldiers and their essentials but also the officers' extravagances.[57]

Again Francis Parkman listed what a soldier of Massachusetts was issued in 1756. "Besides pay, each man to receive a powder-horn, blanket, knapsack (pack), wooden bottle or canteen, a coat and

---

[54] George Bray III, to Brenton C. Kemmer, 1993, "Inventory of Colonel Ephraim Williams after his death in 1755," Author's Private Collections, Houghton Lake, Michigan.

[55] Hawks, 12.

[56] Rea, 202.

[57] Andy Gallup, "Boats Used in the Lake Champlain Campaigns of 1758-1759," *Journal of the Forces of Montcalm and Wolfe* 3 # 2 (1990) 12-16; Dr. David Starbuck, ed.; Joseph W. Zarzynski & John Farrell "Recent Underwater Archaeological Surveys at Lake George, New York," *Military Sites of the Hudson River, Lake George, and Lake Champlain Corridor* (Queensbury, NY: Adirondack Community College, 1995) 5-9.

Fig. 6. Bagley's men were issued great coats, sometimes called watch coats, shown in the foreground. Some men fashioned their own coats from blankets, as shown in the background.

soldier's hat. The coat of coarse blue cloth, to which breeches of red or blue were afterwards added."[58] A deserter report of May 11, 1756, for Thomas Spywood, of Capt. Blake's Company of Bagley's regiment said Spywood went away wearing a blue coat and red waistcoat.[59] Colonel Winslow wrote to Massachusetts Governor William Shirley in the spring of 1756 with a proposal of issued items for the campaign. Winslow says, "each mess should contain six men and be allowed a camp kettle, a bowl, and platter and the officers of each company two, and every man a spoon. That each man be allowed a blanket, knapsack, and bandelet, and the kings arms and accouterments."[60] On November 10, at Fort William Henry, His Majesty's stores received from Colonel Bagley firelocks with bayonets, cartouch boxes, and slings. The colony's *Acts and Resolves* says blankets, powder, and ball had been issued. In some cases the men received blankets or other warm clothing. The House of Representatives spelled out once in 1756 that the soldiers serving at Fort William Henry, where Bagley's men were, received a great coat, blanket, and bed sack. A great coat was a woolen overcoat. These were blanket-weight coats, some having capes over the shoulders for extra warmth. Those soldiers not issued these coats either brought or purchased them, or fashioned a coat from issued blankets (see fig. 6). The bed sack, a colonial canvas sleeping bag, was usually waterproofed and held bedding. A commissary return from June 22, 1756, lists shirts, stockings, shoes, breeches, great coats, stocks, caps, and blankets, all in Massachusetts stores. A December 1756 return from Massachusetts stores in Albany lists sheets, bed sacks, pillows, bags, steelyards, guns, bayonets, drums, case of ball, large brass kettles, and lanthorns (lanthorns were lanterns, a common naval term, and steelyards were instruments for measurement by an uneven scale hung by a hook). In October, Bagley's men received 20 wagons of

---

[58] Parkman, 224-25.

[59] Albert W. Haarmann, "American Uniforms During the French and Indian War, 1754-1763," *Military Collector and Historian* 32 #2 (summer 1980) 58.

[60] Albert B. Hart, ed., *Commonwealth History of Massachusetts*, no. 2 (New York: Russell & Russell), 433.

clothing.[61] These clothes were either late or cold weather clothing for garrison duty in winter. For muskets, the men of the 1756 campaign could bring their own and receive a two-dollar bounty or be supplied a "Brown Bess" musket, also called King's arms.[62] In 1756, the centinels and NCOs must have looked much like the soldiers of the previous year.

Contemporary art gives us a good look at officers' clothing. Joseph Badger of the Boston Militia was painted in his captain's uniform. Badger's uniform bears a striking resemblance to the officers' uniforms worn in the 1740's. The coat has no collar, but large cuffs, and hangs to the knee. The coat, cuffs, waistcoat, and breeches were scarlet. His waistcoat was laced in gold.[63]

The documentation for 1757 is much more detailed than the two previous years. The soldiers received a coat, soldier's hat, knapsack, hatchet, tin kettle, tin flask or canteen, musket, powder horn, bullet pouch, bayonet, and tents. Blankets did not appear in that year's list. One clothing order shows the issued coats were lapelled and were made in small, medium, and large.[64] One way the colony acquired its soldiers' coats was by advertising. On February 23, 1757, the *Boston Weekly News Letter* reported, "the assembly voted to give each NCO and soldier a coat and a hat." Three days later the Committee of War

---

[61] Abercromby Papers, Huntington Library, CA.: Nov. 1995, Nick Westbrook Notes, Fort Ticonderoga, Pell Research Center: #AB874; American Antiquarian Society, "Order for 404 Coats, small, medium, and large, scarlet lapels for officers," 1757, French and Indian War, Manuscript Box, Folder 8, 1756-57 - undated, Worcester, Mass.; "Account, John Burk to Isaac Gridley, Commissary of Col. Dwight's Regt., June 22, 1756; Massachusetts Historical Society, "Acct. of Sundries Returned in Stores by Samuel Livermore Sgt., Albany, Dec. 9, 1756, Misc. Bound, Moses Emerson, Single Sheet, Massachusetts Historical Society, Boston, Mass.

[62] *A&R*, 350, 513-14; Greenleaf, 99.

[63] Cecil C. P. Lawson, *A History of the Uniforms of the British Army*, vol. 2 (London: Peter Davies, 1941), 195; *Military Collector and Historian* 18 #2 (Summer 1991) Plate 669.

[64] American Antiquarian Society, "Order for 404 Coats," French and Indian War, Manuscript Box, Folder 8, 1756-1757-undated.

advertised for "blue cloths, from 3s. to 5s. sterling per yard and red half thicks [sic] or cloths for lapels and cuffs of these coats."[65]

In 1758 the Massachusetts soldiers received a knapsack, tin flask or wooden bottle, muskets, some blankets, and hatchets. In April the *Journal of the House of Representatives* stated each man should furnish his own blanket and arms. Each mess of six men received a tin kettle of ten quarts and a small or light wood ax. The 1758 gear appeared the same except some supplied their own musket, and some supplied their own blanket.[66]

Francis Parkman said that when the English army left to attack Fort Ticonderoga, the provincials were the flank columns uniformed in blue. Cecil Lawson described another painting depicting Capt. Joseph Jackson of Massachusetts in a blue coat and scarlet waistcoat with gold lace on the waistcoat and hat. Evidently there was some issuance of clothing because in October, a Negro of Captain Taplin's company of Bagley's regiment received 75 lashes for selling his clothing.[67]

A number of 1758 inventories of Massachusetts soldiers who died at the Battle of Ticonderoga have survived. They are from Captain Lawrence's company of Colonel Nichols' regiment. They include Captain Lawrence, Sergeants Oliver Wright and Oliver Laking, Corporal Nehemiah Boold, and five centinels. Captain Lawrence's inventory included 1 pr. woolen breeches, 1 ruffled shirt, 1 not ruffled, 1 wig, 2 pr. worsted stockings, 1 pr. shoes, 1 brass ink pot, 1 ribbon for a tie, 1 wooden bottle, 1 razor, 1 trump line, and 1 knapsack. Notice he had less gear than colonels did in earlier years. Rank certainly did have privileges. Between the three NCOs, all had shirts and shoes, two had breeches, stockings, coats, and knapsacks. Other

---

[65] Haarmann, p. 59.

[66] *JHR*, 34 part 2: 417, 419; John Cleaveland to Mary Cleaveland, August 11, 1758, *John Cleaveland Papers* (Salem: Essex Institute, 1974, microfilm), 1; "Amos Richardson's Journal, 1758," *The Bulletin of the Fort Ticonderoga Museum* 12 #4 (May 1979): 271, 281; "Petition of Ruth Farmer, 1758," *The Bulletin of the Fort Ticonderoga Museum* 2 #2 (July 1930): 79; Paul O. Blanchette, ed., *Captain William Sweat's Personal Diary of the Expedition Against Ticonderoga* (Salem: Essex Institute, Historical Collections) vol. 93 (1957) 38-39.

[67] Parkman, 358; Lawson, 195; Sweat, 38-39; Rea, 65.

items of clothing and gear listed were leggings, razor, coat, jacket, waistcoat, trump line, belt, bottle, handkerchief, and specks. Keep in mind these inventories would not include items they were wearing when buried. Some items may also have been missing, and others, not found.

All five centinels had inventoried caps, stockings, leather breeches, and trump lines. Two men owned knapsacks, leggings, and handkerchiefs. Other items in the inventories were breeches, shoes, stock, knife, razor, trousers, bottle, hatchet, and a blanket. These inventories show that the Massachusetts soldiers were supplied with the basics. Some items though, were on their person or stashed during battle, such as blankets, weapons, fire starting kits, and another set of clothing. The items listed were probably duplicate items.[68]

The storage facility and military accommodations were documented by many of the soldiers in 1758. That year the English government wrote that Prime Minister William Pitt was to provide the colonials with ammunition, provisions, and tents.[69] In Bagley's regiment there appeared some complaining about these canvas homes. Joseph Nichols said, "These tents become very uncomfortable."[70] Commonly, Massachusetts regiments, especially Bagley's, set up their camps randomly. They almost seemed to place their tents according to independent pleasure. The provincial soldiers usually had filthy camps, with garbage strewn on the ground, cooking fires and preparation areas with rotting food scraps too close to the privy, uneven ground with low areas filled with standing water, and the stench from the common practice of relieving themselves in company streets. One soldier talked about walking four to five miles away from camp to get away from the smell. Bagley, probably under orders, tried on August 29 of 1758, to clear the air. "The tents of the whole army to be struckt at least once a week and the ground ear'd." [71]

---

[68] "Captain Thomas Lawrence's Company, an Inventory List of Clothing and Gear From Deceased Soldiers," *Massachusetts Historical Society, Proceedings* (Boston: Massachusetts Historical Society, May 1890) 25: 26-29.

[69] John A. Schutz, *Thomas Pownall, British Defender of American Liberty* (California: The Arthur H. Clark Co., 1951) 127.

[70] Nichols, 66.

[71] Bagley, Aug. 21, 1758 (see Appendix 7).

FREEMEN, FREEHOLDERS, AND CITIZEN SOLDIERS

In 1758 flags are mentioned for Massachusetts regiments, this time in Bagley's regiment. When Bagley's troops left Fort Miller, heading north toward Fort Edward and Lake George to prepare for the assault on Fort Ticonderoga, they were partly in bateaux and partly on land. In the lead were Colonel Bagley and Lieutenant Colonel John Whitcomb, with flags flying, and using their blankets for sails (see fig. 7).[72] Often, field officers of the army had a King's colours and regimental colours. The King's colours used primarily in North America was the red ensign. This flag had a red field and a Union Jack in the upper left quarter of the flag. The full Union Jack flag would not have been carried by any but a royal regiment, probably grenadier companies or at fortresses. These silk flags were six feet, six inches long and six feet wide. They were cased on a ten to ten-and-a-half-foot pole for carrying or posting. Few Massachusetts regimental flags remain today. A few are documented to particular units. Bagley's regimental flag was probably the pine tree flag of New England. This flag had either a blue or red field with a red cross on a white field in the upper left quarter. In the upper left of the white segmented field was the pine tree emblem of New England. This New England flag was carried by the military units from 1737 through the next fifty years (see fig. 8).[73]

In 1759, the men received gear which included wooden bottles made with one hoop or a canteen, hatchet, knapsack, blanket, some cartridge boxes or powder horns, and muskets. Each mess of six men was also to receive two tin kettles, each of ten quarts, and a hatchet.[74] The item called a cartridge box was a leather bag containing a wooden block with holes drilled in rows in which to place cartridges. An outer flap of leather fell over the front to keep the powder inside dry (see fig. 9).

---

[72] Nichols, 12.

[73] Flag Research Center of Winchester, Massachusetts, to Brenton C. Kemmer, 1993, Author's Private Collections, Houghton Lake, Michigan; *Flags of America, sesquicentennial edition*, (Philadelphia: The John Wanamaker Store, 1926) 12; George C. Neumann and Frank J. Kravic, *Collector's Illustrated Encyclopedia of the American Revolution*, (Texarkana, Texas: Rebel Publishing Co. Inc., 1989) 86-88.

[74] *JHR*, 274, 287, 335; Hawks, 7; *A&R*, 16: 313.

Fig. 7. Advancing from Ft. Miller toward Ft. Edward and Lake George for the assault on Ticonderoga in 1758. Bagley and Lt. Col. Whitcomb were in the lead of seven bateaux with blankets for sails and their flags flying. The rest of the regiment was to advance on shore.

Fig. 9. Massachusetts soldiers were issued some standard military gear from the King's stores and Massachusetts stores. The cartridge box on the right hip of the soldier in the foreground is a good example.

Fig. 8. Field officers of Massachusetts carried colours during the war. Here is a field officer with the King's Red Ensign and the Pine Tree flag of New England.

Fig 10. In 1759 Bagley's drummers were to be uniformed in green coats. Here in the foreground is one of his drummers.

Fig. 11. The three soldiers above are wearing the 1760 issue uniforms. They are blue broadcloth with colored facings (lapel & cuff), the 1st Regiment in blue, 2nd Regiment in red, and the 3rd in green.

Fig. 12. Bagley's officers sometimes purchased their own uniforms like the field officer on the left. These red, red faced coats were similar to those worn in the 1740's. Company officers were issued blue coats with red facings. Officers commonly laced their uniforms with gold braid.

Fig. 13. David Mason was a commissary lieutenant, and captain in the Massachusetts Provincials during the French and Indian War. Here he is painted in his company officer's uniform. (Reproduced with the permission of the Peabody Essex Museum, Salem, MA.)

FREEMEN, FREEHOLDERS, AND CITIZEN SOLDIERS 47

Colonel Joseph Frye's and Colonel Bagley's regiments were the first into Nova Scotia in 1759. Captain John Knox of the 43rd Regiment of Foot witnessed Frye's landing. "Early this morning arrived Col. Frye of the provincials. They make a decent appearance being clothed in blue faced with scarlet, gilt buttons, laced waistcoats and hats; but the ordinary soldiers have no uniform, nor do they affect any kind of regularity."[75] An advertisement documents Massachusetts regimentals and other clothing for the soldiers, "blue broad cloth, lapelled coats, blue and red half thick breeches, German serge, drugget [sic] and leather ditto, checked and ozanbrig [sic] trousers, checked shirts, and milled and worsted caps."[76] Centinels and NCOs were also issued some shirts, stockings, shoes, great coats, or watch coats. Each regiment received 30 of the previously mentioned coats for guard duty.[77] Another order is very enlightening: "Each man be equipped with a coat, waistcoat and breeches suitable for the campaign, also three good shirts, two good pair of shoes, and two good pair of stockings, and a hat.... Commanding officers are to see their men have hats and to see that none wear trousers, none to wear caps when paraded.... Ye commanding officer desires ye Captains that they would remind it to ye sergeants and corporals of each company that they would provide themselves with blue coats and laced hats and the corporals to have yellow knots on their shoulders and ye drums green coats."[78] (See fig. 10.) Again a similar officer's uniform is captured in art, the only difference is the addition of gold lacing on the coat and hat.[79] The centinels again were almost entirely uniformed this year.

One thing of notice in July of 1759 was a regimental order from Ruggles, "all great hats are to be cut so that the brims be two inches and a half wide and that no man wears a cap under his hat and more

---

[75] Captain John Knox, *The Historical Journal of the Campaigns in North America for the Years 1757, 1758, 1759, and 1760* (Toronto: The Champlain Society, 1914), 1: 306.

[76] Gary Zaboly

[77] *A&R*, 313; Hawks, 11.

[78] Haarmann, p. 59.

[79] *A&R*, 575, 631, 686, 688, 693, 700; *JHR*, 34 part 2: 415; Lawson, 195.

especially when on duty."⁸⁰ This order addressed a layered fashion of wearing a fabric cap under the hat. This may have been for warmth, comfort, or fashion. The cutting of the great hats uniformed some of the head gear and kept it from obstructing the musket.

In 1760, Bagley's regiment and the rest of the Massachusetts troops looked very much like eighteenth-century European soldiers. By this year they not only received good individual gear but cartridge boxes and muskets as well.⁸¹ For clothing the soldiers received full uniforms. Each man got a blue broadcloth lapelled coat. The lapel colors varied by regiment. The first regiment wore blue, the second red, and the third green. Each man received a flannel wool waistcoat and a felt hat bound with white ferret (ribbon, or wool tape) (see fig. 11). Other items issued to Bagley's regiment at Fortress Louisbourg were knapsacks, kettles, mess hatchets, blankets, and bolsters.⁸² In addition, the soldiers sought clothing from their sutlers. Gibson Clough of Bagley's regiment purchased a pair of leather breeches. Another man, a centinel, bought stockings, shoes, a great coat, two shirts; and he sold a red coat he had brought along with him.⁸³

In paintings of 1760, officers again dressed in red coats. Captain John Lanabee wore a scarlet coat and a black waistcoat with crimson breeches. Colonel John Winslow had a scarlet coat and waistcoat laced in gold.⁸⁴

Bagley's soldiers through the years of 1755-1760 would have been clothed similarly to their accustomed style at home. For all of the campaigns, soldiers of Massachusetts-Bay were given the appearance of uniformity. This full military appearance was gradual until 1760. As for Bagley's officers, one would have seen uniforms attempting to imitate the English officer corps. Many young provincial officers

---

[80] Hawks, 19-20.

[81] Hawks, 64; "Journal of Sergeant Holden," *Massachusetts Historical Society, Proceedings*, (Boston: Massachusetts Historical Society, 1899) 388.

[82] *A&R*, 356-57; American Antiquarian Society, "Acct. of the 2nd Billeting Money Which Have Been Paid out and to Whome, As Also Blankets, Knapsacks, etc." French and Indian War Collection, M55 Boxes F, Folder 8.

[83] "Extracts From Gibson Clough's Journal." (Salem: Essex Institute, Historical Collections) 3 (1861) 102; Procter, 57.

[84] Lawson, 195.

FREEMEN, FREEHOLDERS, AND CITIZEN SOLDIERS   49

hoped to become regular English officers. This explains the regularity of red coats and gold lacing, although there was an attempt to uniform field officers in red and company officers in blue as shown in 1759 (see fig. 12). The Peabody Essex Museum of Salem, Massachusetts, has a good oil (painting) of David Mason in his company officer's uniform. He was a commissary in 1755, a lieutenant from 1756-58, 1762, and a captain in 1763. His uniform is dark navy with red lapels. His red waistcoat is laced in gold, as is his soldier's hat. Mason also wears a white shirt and black neck cloth (see fig. 13).[85] Some of the officers wore old uniforms from the previous war (King George's War). Many tried to make a statement of equality with the English.

The English supplied the colony tentage again in 1760. In June, Massachusetts received 21 marquees from the quartermaster of the 27th Regiment of Foot.[86] After several years of government supply, the Bay Colony by 1760 must have been quite regimented to the standardized English-issue tents. This does not mean these were the optimum dwellings. During these war years a provincial term for these tents was "oznaburgs." "We shall soon, I hope be moving homeward, for it begins to be cold nights, and our oznaburg tabernacles are but poor shelters for this cold climate."[87] Oznaburg refers to a thick, coarse-weight linen. The term tabernacle refers not only to the soldiers' religious connotation but sarcastically to the similar portable sanctuaries in which Jews carried the ark of the covenant in the desert.

---

[85] Henry W. Foote, *Portraits in the Essex Institute, Salem* (Salem, MA: Essex Institute, 1936) 127-28; Peabody Essex Museum, Lt. Col. David Mason, 1726-1794 Oil unknown artist, gift of S. Prescott Fay, 130,763, Peabody Essex Museum, Salem, MA; Nancy S. Voye, ed., *Massachusetts Officers in the French and Indian Wars, 1748-1763* (Boston: The New England Historic Genealogical Society, 1975).

[86] Hawks, 64.

[87] "Samuel Jenks, His Journal of the Campaign in 1760," *Massachusetts Historical Society, Proceedings* (Boston: Massachusetts Historical Society, 1890) 5: 375.

Part IV:

OUR DUTY IS SO HARD THAT OUR MEN SCARCELY HAVE TIME TO COOK THEIR VICTUALS OR WASH THEIR CLOTHES

Work around these camps and the forts was strenuous, and the great majority of it fell upon the provincials. The freemen of Bagley's and many other regiments of Massachusetts had a large percentage of skilled woodworkers. These carpenters had their work cut out for them during this war. They felled the trees, hewed the timber, and then constructed the forts and buildings. Fort William Henry was a prime example. In 1756 Bagley had at least three company commanders requesting carpenter's pay of nearly 300 pounds for their men. Again, in 1758, Bagley himself ordered men to finish the hospital, build a guard house, and complete other construction on the new fort on Lake George. Also in 1758 Bagley was in charge of the construction of a bridge just to the south of Fort Edward on the Hudson River. This bridge was called Bagley Bridge and is first mentioned in Gen. Winslow's Orderly Book.[88]

These citizen-soldiers also constructed large numbers of maritime vessels. The main transportation used for gear, equipment, and men were bateaux and whale boats constructed by Massachusetts laborers. These boats mounted batteries of cannon. In 1755, General Johnson ordered Captain Webster of Bagley's regiment to take thirty-six of his carpenters and construct two floating batteries. In 1756, Gen. Winslow ordered Bagley to make ready all sloops, lights, and bateaux at Fort William Henry to proceed to Ticonderoga. During 1758, Capt. Loring of the Royal Navy and Col. Bagley built a ninety-ton sloop mounting fourteen 6 and 4 pounders on Lake George.[89]

---

[88] William Hill, 213; *JHR*, 33 part 1: 52; *Ibid.*, 32 part 2: 435; *A&R*, 15: 454; Bagley, 1, 10.

[89] Harrison Bird, *Navies in the Mountains, The Battles on the Waves of Lake Champlain and Lake George, 1609-1814* (New York: Oxford University Press, 1962) 61; *Francis Parkman Papers*, vol. 42, p. 253-54, Massachusetts Historical Society, State Papers America & West Indies, vol. 87; Gipson, 207.

Bagley's men also built breastworks of stone, timber, and fashines (bundles of sticks), cleared land, cut firewood, made oars, cut hay, fetched water, repaired buildings and forts, escorted wagons and boats with supplies, made shingles, entrenched works, built houses and huts, built wharves, and stood guard duty. This list could go on and on.[90] Joseph Nichols of Bagley's regiment said in 1758, "Our duty is so hard that our men scarcely have time to cook their victuals or wash their clothes."[91]

Training and drilling the soldiers took up time as well. The men had to practice their manual exercise for several reasons. First, they had this type of drill only once a month back home in their militia musters. As freemen, rather than regular standing armies, they were not accustomed to the expected proficiencies. Second, for their own safety and that of their fellow soldiers, the men had to rehearse in the choreography of maneuvering and fighting under extreme conditions with loaded muskets. Bagley's own sergeants were ordered to form into a single rank and, "to be exercised two times a day until trained in their duty."[92] This is not to mean Bagley's troops, although not crack drill experts, became proficient enough for safety, fighting, and periodic exercise inspections, or parading before field officers.[93]

Several other types of drills were also performed. Because of the terrain of the corridors of fighting, these men needed training in bush fighting (guerrilla warfare). Only the frontiersmen and scattered Indians in the ranks knew these fighting strategies. As recorded in his orderly book of 1758, Bagley ordered his troops to make themselves experts at marching and forming in the woods. They practiced this three times a week with the other provincials at Lake George.[94]

The soldiers worked very little at the drill of target practicing. It proved dangerous for many of these city boys and country bumpkins to have loaded weapons. Many had never fired a musket until coming

---

[90] Rea, 33-34, 59; Fred Anderson, to Brenton C. Kemmer, 1994, Miscellaneous Diary Notes, Author's Private Collections, Houghton Lake, Michigan; Greenleaf, 23, 33, 49, 71, 77-78, 89-90, 102-103.

[91] Nichols, 66.

[92] Rea, 23.

[93] *Ibid.*

[94] Rea, 23; Bagley, 5.

to war. Many never fired their musket until actually in battle! Numerous accidental shootings occurred in the camps and on the march. Bagley's troops had every bit of their share of these misfortunes. At least eight men died by accident in Bagley's regiment in 1758 alone.[95]

Doctors were needed in Bagley's regiment. Medical care for accidental and war wounds was extremely important. Men also complained about broken bones, sprains, bruised feet, overheating and cooling, and headaches. These were just some of the complaints while on the march to the battle fronts. Bagley's doctor, Caleb Rea, in 1758 said, "it is so bad of a march it started to have a common saying, no need to pass muster or any other proof of their fitness for a campaign but to march through these woods."[96] Other ailments of Bagley's men included diarrhea, dysentery, scurvy, fever, measles, bloody purge, pains in the limbs and chest, problems with their bowels, and camp fever.[97]

The colony saw to it that each regiment had enlisted a surgeon and two surgeon's mates to assist him. Each received a surgeon's chest filled to his specifications. They also set aside 150 pounds in 1755 and 300 in 1756 for the necessities of the sick and wounded.[98]

Most of Bagley's men's ailments involved disorders of the intestinal tract and bowels. On July 1, 1758, Dr. Rea borrowed some medicines he needed for his medical chest. These items were, "pul. Rhei-one dr.-60 grains (pulverized rhubarb), Crm. Tartar-one oz. (cream of tartar), Laud. Liquid-one oz. (tincture of laudanum), Diascord-one oz. (diascordium), Pil. Cochia-one oz. (cochineal), and Pul. Corte-one oz. (cortex). The rhubarb both settled and purged the stomach, cream of tartar in small doses settled the stomach and in large doses purged, diascordium was used to purge, cochineal was used to purge and also as a muscle relaxant, cortex caused nausea and

---

[95] Rea, 18-19, 47; Nichols, 9; Cleaveland, 195.

[96] Rea, 14-15.

[97] *Ibid.*, 29, 31, 52; Fred Anderson, to Brenton C. Kemmer, 1994, "Enoch Poor Diary Notes," Author's Private Collections, Houghton Lake, Michigan; Nichols, 74; Cleaveland, 200-01.

[98] *JHR*, 30: 294; *Ibid.*, 32 part: 370-72; *Ibid.*, 34 part 2: 445; *Ibid.*, 35: 334; Rea, 15.

vomiting, and the laudanum would settle the stomach in small doses, purge in larger doses, and could be used as a sedative, pain killer or euphoric to simply make the soldiers feel good.[99]

During this period in history, doctors and people in general thought that the body must flush itself of impurities to get rid of illness. This was done in three ways. One way was to bleed, using a specifically designed instrument called a lancet, to cut the patient and allow them to bleed. The second way was to purge or evacuate through the bowels. The third was to vomit the impurities causing the illness. Vomiting, probably by taking cortex, was quite common in this army. Dr. Rea himself took an emetic as did Samuel Greenleaf and the Reverend John Cleaveland.[100]

Dr. Caleb Rea and Reverend Cleaveland both had theories as to the causes of many of these ailments. Rea felt that many grew ill because of the changing weather. Cleaveland thought that many of the illnesses came from being scared, having poor digestion, feeling discouraged, and disappointed, and by drinking lake water.[101] I tend to side with Cleaveland.

---

[99] Rea, 22; Pharmacists Dana Marra and Pat Marra, Interview by Author, April 1994, Houghton Lake, Michigan, Author's Private Collections, Houghton Lake, Michigan; Horatio Wood Jr. and Arthur Osol, *The Dispensary of America* (Philadelphia: 23rd edition, J. B. Lippincott, Co., 1943), 329-331, 309-317; E. S. C. Weiner, *The Oxford English Dictionary* (Oxford: 2nd edition, Clarendon Press, 1989), "Diascord," 4: 613.

[100] Rea, 58; Greenleaf, 61; Cleaveland, 200.

[101] Rea, 58; Cleaveland, 200.

Part V:
PROVISIONS
OR THE FOUR PENCE IN LEU OF IT

Along with the surgeon and two mates, the Massachusetts troops also could call upon the services of women called "camp followers," who would work as nurses or surgeon's mate's assistants. These women had many camp duties. They nursed the ill, washed and sewed clothes, cooked meals, and periodically saw to the soldier's mental and physical needs. For pay they received one-half a ration of food or, as was offered in 1760, four pence a month. These women followed the army also as wives to some of the soldiers, officers, and sutlers. Early in the war, the camp followers were usually seen as a burden and sent home, as Gen. William Johnson did in 1755. By the end of the war, women appeared more in the encampments of Massachusetts-Bay.[102] At Nova Scotia in 1760 Captain Jenks noted in his orderly book about the camp ladies coming into camp. He also noted the poor treatment of a sutler's woman and of losing two shirts to a wash woman.[103] Sergeant Holden of Massachusetts documents a woman who belonged to Captain Hutchings' company (of Massachusetts), "brought a bed with a stately soldier for the king." The sergeant also stated that on June 1, 1760, "that the regiments of 1,000 should be allowed, provisions or the four pence in leu of it, for four women per company and those of 700 for 3 women per company."[104]

Victualling records of December 10, 1759 through January 6, 1760 of Col. Bagley's provincial regiment stationed at Fortress Louisbourg show a good breakdown of followers in his distaff. Capt.

---

[102] "Journal of Captain Eleazer Melvin's Co., Shirley's Expedition, 1754," *New England Historic Genealogical Register,* vol. 27(1873) 109; Walter H. Blumenthal, *Women Camp Followers of the American Revolution* (Salem, New Hampshire: Ayer Company, Publishers, Inc., 1988) 45-51; Linda G. DePauw, *Founding Mothers, Women in America in the Revolutionary Era* (Boston: Houghton Mifflin Co., 1975) 179-180.

[103] Jenks, 354, 364, 367.

[104] "Journal of Sergeant Holden," *Massachusetts Historical Society, Proceedings* (Boston: Massachusetts Historical Society, 1889) 24: 388, 391.

Moore's company had 49 centinels and no followers; Capt. Hanner's company had 44 centinels and 6 followers; Capt. Davis' company had 51 centinels and 4 followers; Capt. George's company had 46 centinels and 2 followers; Capt. Newhall's company had 48 centinels and 4 followers; Capt. Gridding's company had 52 centinels and no followers; Capt. Glover's company had 51 centinels and 3 followers; Capt. Blake's company had 48 centinels and 4 followers; and Capt. Chudburn's company had 42 centinels and no followers (most of these companies had 4 sergeants, 4 corporals, and 2 drummers). This lists Bagley's nine-company garrison as having 431 centinels and 23 followers. According to these records Bagley's regiment had a higher ratio of followers than most English regiments. By far the majority of the followers in Bagley's regiment were related to men in the regiment. Out of the twenty-one surnames listed for followers, fifteen were surnames of men in their listed companies. Seventy-four percent of Bagley's followers were relatives of soldiers in the regiment.[105] (see fig. 14.)

---

[105] B. A. Balcom, Historian, Fortress of Louisbourg National Historic Site, to Brenton C. Kemmer Dec. 19, 1994, "Victualing Lists of Col. Bagley's Regiment, Dec. 10, 1759 - Jan. 6, 1760, Photocopy, Kemmer Private Collection, Houghton Lake, Michigan.

Fig. 14. Camp followers were rarely in the Massachusetts camps in the early war but by 1759-1760 each company was allowed three to four, depending on their company's size.

Part VI:

WHEN I GET OUT OF THEIR POWER I SHALL TAKE CARE HOW I GET IN AGAIN

Religion was not necessarily brought to these Bay Colony soldiers of Bagley's regiment by the women followers or the chaplains, but for many it came from a deeply rooted Puritan and Congregationalist faith. Some of these men came from pockets of the Bay Colony that still emphasized their religious piety. The colony itself even made sure each regiment had a chaplain in each campaign. These leaders in their Geneva collars helped many to deal with the mental anguish and disturbance of warfare. Colonel Bagley ordered his captains in 1758 to attend services twice a day at 6 a.m. and 7 p.m. Reverend John Cleaveland, Bagley's 1758-59 chaplain, called for the best four or five singers of each company to sing psalms at services.[106] This does not mean that all of the men in the regiment were devout, but rather that a large group did strive for piety, while others struggled with it, some hypocritically worshipped, and others ignored religion. Dr. Rea spoke several times in his journal about soldiers of Bagley's regiment profaning the Sabbath by playing cards or coppers, swearing and cursing, and playing and singing music. He also said that this profaning included the officers of the regiment as well. "Sad! Sad! is it to see how the Sabbath is profaned in ye camp!"[107]

This lack of religion on the part of some, along with the hypocritical behavior of others, showed up in the disobedience of the troops. Some of Bagley's men killed cattle, refused to do duties, stole items, deserted, mutinied, swore, disobeyed orders, quarreled with superiors, threatened others' lives, sold liquor without a license, and made general disturbances. Punishments ranged from repenting that one would not do it again to death. The most common punishments in Bagley's regiment were flogging with a cat-of-nine-tails and "riding the wooden horse." A regimental court determined one's guilt, and if guilty, this court of officers of Bagley's regiment prescribed the

---

[106] Cleaveland, 193; Rea, 18.

[107] Rea, 13, 18, 36.

punishment according to the *Articles of War*. Periodically, sentences would be lowered by their commander. For killing cattle, the men were sentenced 50 lashes, but only received 10 each; for denying one's duty, some men rode the wooden horse, and some were confined in the guard house; for theft, punishment could range from 100 lashes to death; for bad conduct, a man could get 50 lashes, or ride the wooden horse; for mutiny, 500 lashes if a few men offended, or in the case of about 150 men of Bagley's in 1760, confinement for one day; for talking severely to his superior, a lieutenant had his sword broken over his head and he was banished from camp; for threatening the life of another man, one received 30 lashes; for swearing, one could receive 100 lashes; for desertion, one received 200 lashes and was drummed out of the regiment; and for threatening an officer, one could receive 200 lashes. The centinels were not the only soldiers in Bagley's regiment to do wrong. Twice in 1758 Bagley's sergeants and corporals were confined for neglecting their duties.[108] As Joseph Nichols said in 1758, "hard service and poor keeping make Jack a dull boy."[109]

This debauchery of disobedience involved not the masses of Bagley's soldiery, but only the minority of disillusioned, ill-kept sluggards who usually pulled down the rest of society. The majority of Colonel Jonathan Bagley's men held in their hearts the remembrance of their families, homes, colony, and country, and strove with every exertion capable to drive what they enumerated as the devil papists from North America. One way we witness their sincerity comes from their practice of drinking an evening toast to their wives and sweethearts.[110] These men built, moved, defended, and characterized this conflict for six years, facing poor rations, worn-out clothing, nature's elements, belligerent redcoat officers, and death.

With stresses from lack of food, extended duty, physical exhaustion, and redcoat animosities, Bagley's freeborn Englishmen gradually became fed up. By late war (1759-60), whole groups of his

---

[108] Bagley, Aug. 23, 1758; Rea, 16, 65, 70; Nichols, 30, 79, 99; Hill, 64, 77; Melvin, 30; Pomeroy, 106; Greenleaf, June 14-15, 1756; Cleaveland, 229; Procter, 32, 41-43; Clough, 102, 104-105

[109] Nichols, 50.

[110] Jenks, 356-358, 360-61, 362, 364-66.

regiment were grumbling with disobedience. This is not to say they did not perform their soldierly functions, but they had been driven to united group action. This collective action had its origins in seafaring labor. During the eighteenth century maritime workers, working collectively, being fully dependant on each others' actions, developed massed work stoppages as a viable successful action both on the docks and wharves and shipboard. By the end of the 1760's it even became known as a strike because of sailors striking the sails of a ship to cripple commerce. The men felt their contracts had been breached. They were being used as the army's work horses, being kept beyond their enlistments, and being ill treated by redcoat officers. Discouragement also was taking its toll. Gibson Clough of Bagley's regiment recorded his desperate feelings.[111] "I think it is very probable we shall be here another Campaign and if so we shall be called old soldiers by that time as well as bad rogues and lazy fellows for that is said of all them who serve either King or Country now a days."[112]

---

[111] Marcus Rediker, *Between the Devil and the Deep Blue Sea* (Cambridge, MA.: Cambridge University Press, 1987), 96 &110.
[112] Clough, 102.

Between October and November of 1759 Bagley's regiment had finally had enough. Bagley's entire regiment was confined for refusing to do their duty! It was also during this time that Clough pointedly stated that he no longer wanted to be at Louisbourg. His words give a good insight into the provincial Massachusetts soldier's feelings about redcoats:

> *So the month spends away and cold weather is coming on apace which will make us to look round about us and put in our Winter Clothing and we shall stand in need of good Liquors for to keep up our Spirits on cold days, and we being here within Stone walls are not likely to get Liquors or Cloathes at this time of ye year and although we be Englishmen Born yet we are debarred Englishmens Liberty therefore we now see what it is to be under Martial Law and to be with ye regulars who are but little better than slaves to their Officers; and when I get out of their power I shall take care how I get in again.*[113]

Certainly one can place one's self in the shoes of these freeborn Englishmen, sleeping in their "oznaburg tabernacles," eating salt pork, flour, and rum every day, wearing woolen clothing day after day, struggling to make time to even cook their meager food or mend and wash their tattered uniforms. Besides these daily duties, they had to build and repair fortresses on the frontier of another colony, and brave the attacks of their work and escort parties from heathen savages in league with the French. Then, of course, they must do face-to-face battle with the enemy as a regular force against their militia or push them from a European-style stone fortress. It was no wonder Dieskau saw what he did in the men at the Battle of Lake George.

The tremendous level of camaraderie of this unit, stemming from its blood relations, residency, and shared emotion was overwhelming. These soldiers and camp followers were not strangers to each other, but fathers, sons, brothers, wives, daughters, and neighbors. Many shared their civilian life in occupations as artisans, laborers, husbandman, sailors, carpenters, and freeholders. These men of

---

[113] Clough, 104.

Bagley's regiment had worked together on the wharves, in the towns, and at the meeting houses.

Bagley's regiment, thrust into a foreign terrain with less than adequate food, clothing, gear, and medical care, fared quite well considering they formed part of the backbone of the English army in North America. Their camaraderie, religious background of intolerance, hard work ethic, and fortitude allowed these Yankees to survive and proliferate the character that has embedded itself in continuing generations of revolutionaries and Tories. One need not stop in the eighteenth century to find the influence of these men of Bagley's regiment of the Massachusetts-Bay Colony. They are our character.

> *Every man therefore that wishes to secure his own freedom, and thinks it his duty to defend that of his country, should as he prides himself in being a free citizen, think it his truest honor to be a soldier citizen. It is the right, privilege and pre-eminence of a free citizen to bear arms in the bands of his country.*[114]

---

[114] *The Exercise for the Militia Of the Province of the Massachusetts-Bay, By Order of His Excellency.* Printed and Sold by John Draper & Printers for His Excellency the Captain-General, &c. 1758, Boston, p. 3, Early American Imprints 1639-1800 Supplement, Dr. Clifford K. Shipton editor, Evans Collection #40981, American Antiquarian Society, Worcester, Mass., microprint, 1968.

Appendix 1:

RANGE OF AGE FOR SOLDIERS
Colonel Jonathan Bagley's Regiment, 1756

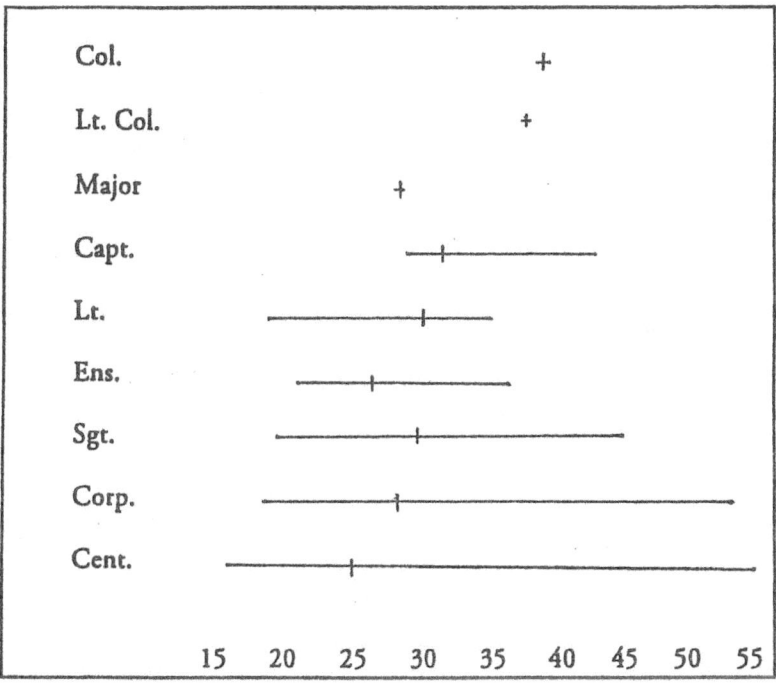

Appendix 2:
Facsimile Officer's Commission, Jonathan Bagley's Regiment

Province of the   Thomas Pownall Esq;

Massachusetts=Bay

Captain General and Governor in Chief, in and over His Majesty's Province of the Massachusetts-Bay in New-England, and Vice-Admiral of the same.

To   Greeting.

By *Virtue of the Power and Authority in and by His Majesty's Royal Commission to Me granted to be Captain General over this His Majesty's Province of the Massachusetts Bay aforesaid-I do by these Presents (reposing especial Trust and Confidence in your Loyalty, Courage and good Conduct) constitute and appoint You the said*   *to be*   *of Jonathan Bagley's Battalion of the Regiment of Foot where Timothy Ruggles Esq. Brigadeer General raised by me to be employed in his Majesty's Service this insuing Campaign.*

You are therefore carefully and diligently to discharge the Duty of   in leading, ordering and exercising said Battalion in Arms both inferior Officers and soldiers and to keep them in good Order and Discipline and they are hereby commanded to obey you as their   and you are yourself to observe and follow such orders and Instructions, as you shall from time to time recieve from the General and Commander in Chief of His Majesty's Forces in North America, your Colonel or other Superior Officer according to His Majesty's Discipline of War Government to the trust hereby found in you.

Given under Hand and Seal at Arms at BOSTON, the   Day of In the   Year of the Reign of His Majesty King GEORGE the Second, Annoq; Domini

By His EXCELLENCY'S   *Regimental Commander*
command

Appendix 3:
Facsimile Impressment Orders

Province of the
Maſſachuſetts-Bay

By His Excellency
William Shirley, Eſq.

Captain-General and Governour in Chief in and over the Province aforeſaid,

To   Eſq; Major of

a Regiment in the County of   Greeting.

WHEREAS the Quota of Men for this Province in the Expedition againſt *Crown-Point*, was by the Reſolves of the Great and General Court, paſſed on the Fourth Day of *March 1756*, determined to be Three Thouſand Five Hundred Men, including Officers, and it is enacted by an Act of ſaid Court paſſed on the Thirteenth Day of *April* laſt, that if the ſaid Number of Men ſhould not be inliſted before the Twenty-ſecond Day of ſaid *April*, it ſhall and may be lawful to compleat the ſame by Impreſs: And whereas notwithſtanding the ſeveral Warrants which have been iſſued by Myſelf and the Lieutenant-Governour in the Time of my Abſence out of the Province, for compleating the aforeſaid Thirty-five Hundred Levies including Officers, purſuant to the ſaid Act, Six Hundred Men are ſtill wanting to compleat the ſame;

NOW you are required forthwith to impreſs
         Men out of your Regiment, and to commit them to an Officer to conduct them to   , in order to their being muſtered, &c. Hereof fail not, and make due Return of your Doings on this Warrant, as you will anſwer your Failure at your Peril.

*Given under my Hand and Seal this   Day of
        Auguſt 1756, in the Thirtieth Year of His Majeſty's Reign.*

Appendix 4:
Bagley's Regiment
A Colonial Listing of Wages

1755

Rank	Pounds	Shillings	Pence
Col.	12	16	0
Lt. Col.	10	13	4
Major	9	1	4
Capt.	4	16	0
Lt.	3	4	0
Ens.	2	2	8
Sgt.	1	14	1
Corp.	1	9	10
Cent.	1	6	8

1756

Rank	Pounds	Shillings	Pence
Col.	12	16	0
Lt. Col.	10	13	4
Major	9	1	4
Capt.	5	8	0
Lt.	3	12	0
Ens.	2	8	0
Sgt.	1	18	4
Corp.	1	13	6
Cent.	1	12	0

1757-1758

Rank	Pounds	Shillings	Pence
Col.	18	0	0
Lt. Col.	15	0	0
Major	12	0	0
Capt.	8	0	0
Lt.	5	0	0
Ens.	3	10	0
Sgt.	2	3	1
Corp.	1	18	7
Cent.	1	16	0

1759-1760

Rank	Pounds	Shillings	Pence
Col.	25	0	0
Lt. Col.	16	13	4
Major	13	6	8
Capt.	9	0	0
Lt.	5	0	0
Ens.	3	10	0
Sgt.	2	3	1
Corp.	1	18	7
Cent.	1	16	0

Per-month 1991 Money Equivalence

Rank	1755	1756	1757	1758	1759	1760
Col.	896	896	1,200	1,140	1,333	1,416
Lt.Col.	745	745	1,000	950	888	944
Major	634	634	800	760	711	755
Capt.	336	336	533	506	480	510
Lt.	224	224	333	316	266	283
Ens.	149	149	233	221	186	198
Sgt.	119	119	143	136	114	122
Corp.	104	104	128	122	102	109
Cent.	93	93	120	114	96	102

Appendix 5:

DEMOGRAPHIC and SERVICE INFORMATION OF THE COMMAND STRUCTURE OF BAGLEY'S REGIMENT, 1755-1762

Compiled by Brenton C. Kemmer - from "Massachusetts Officers in the French and Indian Wars, 1748-1763," Nancy Voye, ed.; Artemas Ward Manuscript, vol. 2, Massachusetts Historical Society, "Victualing Account 1756 & 58;" B.A. Balcom, Historian, Fortress of Louisbourg National Historic Site, to Brenton C. Kemmer, Dec. 19, 1994, "Victualing Lists of Col. Bagley's Regiment, Dec. 10, 1759 - Jan. 6, 1760," Kemmer Private Collection, Houghton Lake, MI.

1755 - 1762
Ft. William Henry, Ft. Edward, Lake George, Nova Scotia

Name & Rank	Residence	Service Time	Place of Service	Company
Col. Jonathan Bagley	Amesbury, MA	1755-1762	Ft. Wm.Hy., Ft. Ed., Louisbourg, A. Alarm List, Canada	own
Lt. Col. & Capt. John Kingsbury	Newbury, MA	1756	Ft. Wm.Hy., Cr. Pt.	own
Lt. Col. & Lt. John Whitcomb	Boston, MA	1756-1758	Canada	own
Lt. Col. William Arbuthnot	---	1760	Louisbourg	own
Lt. Col. Andrew Cole	---	1762	---	own
Major Bensley Glazier	---	1755-56	Ft. Wm.Hy.	own
Major Stephen Miller	Milton, MA	1756-57	Ft. Wm.Hy., Cr.Pt.	own
Major Joseph Ingersoll	Boston, MA	1758	Canada	own
Major Joseph Goldthwait	---	1760-61	Louisbourg	own
Capt. ---- Houghton	---	1756	---	own
Capt. Hesekiel Hutchins	---	1756	---	own
Capt. Thomas Pike	Newbury, MA	1755	Cr. Pt.	own
Capt. Stephen Sargent	---	1756-57	---	own
Capt. ---- Tapley	---	1756	---	own
Capt. John Taplin	Southborough, MA	1756-1759	Ft. Wm.Hy., Ft. Ed., Alarm List, Canada	own
Capt. Stephen Webster	Salisbury, MA	1756	Ft. Wm.Hy.	own
Capt. Stephen Whipple	Ipswich, MA	1758-61	Louisbourg, Canada	own
Capt. Asa Whitcomb	---	1758-59	---	own
Capt. Gideon Woodwell	---	1756	---	own
Capt. Benaiah Young	Newbury, MA	1756	Ft. Wm.Hy., Ft. Ed.	own
Capt. Nathaniel Blake	Milton, MA	1756	Ft. Wm.Hy., Ft. Ed.	own
Capt. Stephen Blake	---	---	---	own
Capt. Israel Davis	Topsfield & Danvers MA	1756-1761	Ft. Wm.Hy., Ft. Ed., Canada	own
Capt. Samuel George	Amesbury, MA	1756-61	Ft. Wm.Hy., Ft. Ed., Louisboug, Alarm List	own

FREEMEN, FREEHOLDERS, AND CITIZEN SOLDIERS

Name & Rank	Residence	Service Time	Place of Service	Company
Capt. Andrew Fuller	Middleton, MA	1758-59	Canada	own
Capt. Andrew Giddinge (Gidding)	Gloucester, MA	1758-59	Canada	own
Capt. Ebenezer Marrow	Medford, MA	1758	Canada	own
Capt. Edmund Moore	Haverhill, MA	1758-61	Canada	own
Capt. Joseph Newhall	Newbury, MA	1758-61	Canada, Louisbourg	own
Capt. Salmon Whitney	Littleton, MA	1758	Canada	own
Capt. Edward Blake	----	1760-61	Louisbourg	own
Capt. Samuel Glover	----	1760-61	Louisbourg	own
Capt. George Hanners	Boston, MA	1759	Louisbourg	own
Capt. Joseph Moody	Falmouth, MA	1760-61	Louisbourg	own
Lt. John Baker	----	1759-61	Louisbourg	Stephen Whipple
Lt. Jonathan Barron	Chelmsford, MA	1755	----	Benaiah Young
Lt. Timothy Colby	Amesbury, MA	1755-56 &59-60	Ft. Wm. Hy., Louisbourg	John Kingsbury
Lt. Nathaniel Ingersoll	Falmouth, MA	1755-58	Canada	John Taplin Joseph Ingersoll
Lt. Samuel Long	Newbury, MA	1755-56	Cr. Pt.	Stephen Sergent
Lt. Samuell Runells	Boxford, MA	1755	Cr. Pt.	Edmund Mooers
Lt. Stephen Whipple	Ipswich, MA	1755	Cr. Pt.	John Whipple
Lt. Philips White	----	1755	Cr. Pt.	Thomas Pike
Lt. James Andrews	Boxford, MA	1756	Ft. Wm. Hy., Cr. Pt.	Israel Davis
Lt. John Bagley	Amesbury, MA	1756-57	Ft. Wm. Hy., Cr. Pt. Alarm list	Samuel George Jonathan Bagley George Wothin
Lt. Benjamin Bridge	Lexington, MA	1756	Ft. Wm. Hy.	Thomas Hartwell
Lt. Ebenezer Brown	Waltham, MA	1756	Ft. Wm. Hy., Cr. Pt.	Timothy Houghton
Lt. Ebenezer Cox	Wrentham, MA	1756-57	Ft. Wm. Hy., Cr. Pt.	Stephen Miller
Lt. Josiah Fay	Southborough, MA	1756	Cr. Pt.	John Taplin
Lt. Jonathan Fessenden	Braintree, MA	1756	Ft. Wm. Hy., Cr. Pt.	Nathaniel Blake
Lt. Samuel George	Amesbury, MA	1756	Cr. Pt.	Jonathan Bagley
Lt. Samuel Greenleaf	Newbury, MA	1756	Ft. Wm. Hy., Cr. Pt.	Benaiah Young
Lt. Hezekiah Hutchins	Newbury, MA	1756	Ft. Wm. Hy., Cr. Pt.	Stephen Miller
Lt. Benjamin Kingsberry (Kingsbury)	Newbury, MA	1756	Ft. Wm. Hy., Cr. Pt.	John Kingsbury
Lt. Thomas Stevens	Amesbury, MA	1756	Ft. Wm. Hy.	Stephen Webster
Lt. Daniel Tucker	Falmouth, Boston, MA	1755-56	Ft. Wm. Hy., Cr. Pt.	Joseph Ingersoll
Lt. Gideon Woodwell	Newbury, MA	1755-57	Ft. Wm. Hy., Cr. Pt.	John Kingsbury Israel Davis
Lt. Benjamin Balch	Scituate, MA	1757	Ft. Wm. Hy.	William Arburthnott
Lt. Joseph Blake	----	1757	----	Ingersoll
Lt. Joel Bradford	Taunton, MA	1757	Ft. Wm. Hy.	William Arburthnott
Lt. James Carr	Woburn, MA	1757	Ft. Wm. Hy.	Israel Davis
Lt. David Titcomb	Newbury, MA	1757	Ft. Wm. Hy.	Israel Davis
Lt. Nathaniel Baily	Gloucester, MA	1758	Canada	Andrew Giddings
Lt. Samuel Burditt	Malden, MA	1758	Canada	Ebenezer Marrow
Lt. Nathan Burnam	Ipswich, MA	1758	Canada	Stephen Whippell
Lt. Peter Carlton	Haverhill, MA	1758	Canada	Edmund Mooers
Lt. Judah Clark	Harvard, MA	1758	Canada	Salmon Whitney
Lt. Darius Green	Malden, MA	1758	Canada	Ebenezer Marrow
Lt. Archelous Fuller	Middleton, MA	1758	Canada	Andrew Fuller

FREEMEN, FREEHOLDERS, AND CITIZEN SOLDIERS 73

Name & Rank	Residence	Service Time	Place of Service	Company
Lt. Benjamin Hastings	Boston, MA	1758-59	Canada	Asa Whitcomb
Lt. Hezekial Hutchins	Newbury, MA	1756-58	Ft. Wm. Hy., Cr. Pt.	Stephen Miller
Lt. Israel Hutchinson	Danvers, MA	1758	---	Andrew Fuller
Lt. Joseph Ilsley	Newbury, MA	1758	Canada	Joseph Newhall
Lt. Nathaniel Ingersoll	Falmouth, MA	1755-58	Canada	John Taplin, Joseph Ingersoll
Lt. Stephen Low	---	1758	Canada	Stephen Whippell
Lt. Isaac Martin	Ipswich, MA	1758-61	Canada, Louisbourg	Andrew Giddings
Lt. Jonathan Pearson	Newbury, MA	1755&58	Cr. Pt., Canada	John Kingsbury, Joseph Newhall
Lt. Richard Sykes	Boston, MA	1758	Canada	Stephen Whippell
Lt. Francis Temple	Newbury, MA	1758-59	Cr. Pt., Canada	Asa Whitcomb
Lt. Leonard Whiting	Westford, MA	1758	Canada	Salmon Whitney
Lt. Edward Emerson	Danvers, MA	1759	Canada	Israel Davis
Lt. Waldo Henderson	---	1759-60	Louisbourg	Andrew Giddings
Lt. Edward Hopkins	Boston, MA	1759-61	Louisbourg	Edward Blake
Lt. Benjamin Kimball	Ipswich, MA	1759	Eastward	Israel Davis
Lt. Enoch Poor	Andover, MA	1759-61	Louisbourg	Samuel Glover
Lt. William Greenleaf	Haverhill, MA	1759-61	Louisbourg	Edmund Mooers
Lt. Thomas Emerson	---	1759-61	---	Joseph Newhall
Lt. Isaac Tuckerman	Boston, MA	1759-61	Louisbourg	George Hanners, Joseph Newhall
Lt. Michael Martin	Boston, MA	1759-61	Louisbourg	George Hanners
Lt. Abraham Tuckerman	Boston, MA	1759-61	Louisbourg	George Hanners
Lt. Humphrey Bradsteet	---	1759&60	Louisbourg	Samuel Glover
Lt. John Burrill	Lynn, MA	1760	---	Israel Davis
Lt. Samuel Knowlton	Ipswich, MA	1759-61	Louisbourg	Stephen Whippell
Lt. John Baker	---	1761	Louisbourg	Stephen Whippell
Lt. Nathan Baker	Haverhill, MA	1761	Louisbourg	Edmund Mooers
Lt. William Taylor	Boston, MA	1760-61	Louisbourg	George Hanners
Lt. Joseph Buck	---	1758	---	---
Lt. Nathan Brigham	---	1758	---	---
Lt. Thomas Colby	---	1758	---	---
Lt. Joshua Moody	---	1759	---	---
Lt. Johnson Moulton	---	1759	---	---
Lt. Edmund Brown	---	1759	---	---
Lt. Samuel Reed	---	1759	---	---
Lt. Ames Williams	---	1759	---	---
Ens. Samuel George	Amesbury, MA	1755	Cr. Pt.	Stephen Sergent
Ens. Philip Lord	---	1755	Cr. Pt.	Stephen Whipple
Ens. Abiel Messer	Methuen, MA	1758	Canada	Edmund Mooers
Ens. Benjamin Swett	---	1755	Cr. Pt.	John Kingsbury
Ens. Timothy Colby	Amesbury, MA	1756-57	Ft. Wm. Hy.	John Kingsbury
Ens. William Cox	Waltham, MA	1756	Cr. Pt.	Timothy Houghton
Ens. Elisha Cummings	Topsfield, MA	1756	Ft. Wm. Hy.	Israel Davis
Ens. Abraham Gale	Weston, MA	1756-57	Ft. Wm. Hy., Cr. Pt.	John Taplin
Ens. Edward Glover	Milton, MA	1756	Ft. Wm. Hy., Cr. Pt.	Nathaniel Blake
Ens. Jonathan Keny	Stoughton, MA	1756	Ft. Wm. Hy.	Stephen Miller
Ens. Moses Prince	Newton, MA	1756	Ft. Wm. Hy., Cr. Pt.	Timothy Houghton
Ens. Josiah Sergant	Amesbury, MA	1756	---	Stephen Webster
Ens. Gilbert Thornton	---	1756	Cr. Pt.	Thomas Hartwell
Ens. Daniel Wheelwright	Wells, MA	1756	Ft. Wm. Hy., Cr. Pt.	Joseph Ingersoll

Name & Rank	Residence	Service Time	Place of Service	Company
Ens. Samuel Williams	Milton, MA	1756-57	Ft. Wm. Hy., Cr. Pt.	Nathaniel Blake
Ens. Joseph Greenleaf	Newbury, MA	1757-58	Ft. Wm. Hy.	Israel Davis
				Joseph Ingersoll
Ens. Samuel Bacon	Medford, MA	1758	Canada	Ebenezer Marrow
Ens. William Bagley	----	1758	Canada	----
Ens. Samuel Davis	Gloucester, MA	1758	Canada	Andrew Giddings
Ens. Samuel Knowlton	Ipswich, MA	1758	Canada	Stephen Whipple
Ens. Zachariah Longley	Groton, MA	1758-59	Canada	Asa Whitcomb
Ens. Isaac Lovejoy	Andover, MA	1758	Canada	Salmon Whitney
Ens. Abiel Messer	Methuen, MA	1758	Canada	Edmund Mooers
Ens. Pearly Pike	Newbury, MA	1758	Canada	Joseph Newhall
Ens. Daniel Porter	Wenham, MA	1758	Canada	Stephen Whipple
Ens. Thomas Trowbridge	Framingham, MA	1758	Canada	John Taplin
Ens. John Holt	----	1758	----	----
Ens. Josiah Berry	Falmouth, MA	1759-61	Louisbourg	Joshua Moody
Ens. John Burril	Lynn, MA	1759	Westward	Israel Davis
Ens. Elisha Hewes	Ipswich, MA	1759-60	Louisbourg	Stephen Whipple
Ens. William McElroy	Marblehead, MA	1759-61	----	Samuel Glover
				Edward Blake
Ens. William Taylor	Boston, MA	1759-61	Louisbourg	George Hanners
Ens. Caleb Woodberry	----	1759	----	Andrew Giddings
Ens. Benjamin Ingersoll	----	1759	----	----
Ens. John Lord	----	1759	----	----
Ens. John Roundey	----	1759	----	----
Ens. Dummer Sewall	----	1759	----	----
Ens. Josiah Woodbury	----	1759	----	----
Ens. Timothy Barnard	Ansbury, MA	1759-60	----	Samuel George
Ens. Benjamin Ingalls	Andover, MA	1759-60	----	Edmund Mooers
Ens. Alexander Mcleod	Boston, MA	1760-61	Louisbourg	Israel Davis
Ens. William M'cleroy	Marblehead, MA	1760-61	Louisbourg	Samuel Glover

Appendix 6:
COMMAND STRUCTURE OF BAGLEY'S BATTALIONS 1755-1762

Compiled by Brenton C. Kemmer - from *Massachusetts Officers in the French and Indian Wars, 1748-1763*, edited by Nancy S. Voye; *Massachusetts Officers and Soldiers in the French and Indian Wars 1755-1756*, edited by K. David Gross and David Zarowin; "Journal of Rev. John Cleaveland, June 14-October 25, 1758," John Cleaveland Papers, microfilm; *The Fort Ticonderoga Museum Bulletin* 10 #3, (1959) 234-236; *Acts and Resolves, Private and Public of Mass.-Bay*, 15: 631; Massachusetts Historical Society, Artemas Ward Manuscript, vol. 2, "1758, victualing account;" Correspondence with B.A. Balcom, Historian, Fortress of Louisbourg, National Historic Site, Louisbourg, Canada, Public Records Office Archival Materials, Canada, "Victualling Records Col. Jonathan Bagley's Regiment, 10 Dec. 1759 - 6 Jan. 1760."

1755
Ft. William Henry, Ft. Edward

Col. Jonathan Bagley

Major Bensley Glazier

Capt. John Burk, John Kingsbury, John Taplin, Thomas Pike, Stephen Sergent, Stephen Webster, John Whipple, Asa Whitcomb, Benaiah Young

Lt. John Baker, Jonathan Barron, Timothy Colby, Nathaniel Ingersoll, Samuel Long, Jonathan Pearson, Samuell Runells, Stephen Whipple, Philips White, Gideon Woodwell

Ens. Samuel George, Philip Lord, Abiel Messer, Benjamin Swett

Adj. John Whiteing, **Clk.** John Appleton, **Clk.** Thomas Clark, **Comm.** William Taylor, **Overseer** John Kingsbury, **Surg.** Amos Putnam, **Surg. Mate** Benjamin Gavitt

Sgt. William Babb, John Campbell, Timothy Colbey, Ebenezer Collings, Aaron Day, Antipas Dodge, Paul Gamatt, Mathia Hoyt, Eliezer Hudson, Ebenezer Knolton, Samuel Smith

Corp. John Attwood, Andrew Downes, David Eaton, Anthony Felton, Isaac Hovey, Nathaniel Lowe, Thomas Saunders, Jacob Smith, William Smith, Nathan Thompson, Charles Trafton

Drum. Phillip Serjeant, Robert Potter, Peter Hay, Nathaniel Getchell

Centinel (*= carpenter) *George Adams, Nathaniel Adams, James Allan, John Badger, Winthrop Bagley, *Anthony Bele, Anthony Bell, *Ebenezer Bishop, Jedediah Blana, Samuel Brown, Stephen Brown, Thomas Brown, Ebenezer Buck, *Joseph Buckley, Gershom Burbank, Israel Burbank, James Burt, Joseph Buswell, Thomas Butman, Charles Casaday, Daniel Cheyney, Jonas Clay, Phillip Colbey, *Timothy Colbey, Timothy Colbey Jr., *Phillip Colbie, *Timothy Colbie, Philip Coleby, Timothy Coleby, John Cooper, Joseph Cooper, Moses Cross, *Samuel Dalton, John Daniels, *Edmund Davis, Ezekiel Davis, Increase Davis, Moses Davis, Ebenezer Davise, *Aaron Day, John Dennis, Joseph Dill, Israel Dodge, Samuel Dolten, Gideon Donnes, *Jon. Dustan, Jonathan Dustan Jr., *Jonathan Dustan, Samuel Eastman, *Thomas Eaton, *Peter English, Peter English, Mark Fisk, John Folemsbey, Samuel Foot, James Fowler, James French, John Frenk, *Paul Garuatt, Israel Gardner, Samuel George Jr., Samuel George, Nathaniel Gilmore, Joseph Goe, Bartholimew Goier, Phinehas Graves, *Thomas Greenleaf, Thomas Greenleaf, *John Hacket, John Hacket, Theodore Hacket, Thes. Hacket, Joseph Hadlock, *John Harkness, Ebenezer Hart, *Jacob Harvey, Jacob Harvey, Joseph Harvey, Thomas Haws, John Hay, Nathaniel Heard, Nathaniel Hill, Moses Hodgskins, *John Holliday, John Holliday, John Howles, Jacob Hoyt, Theodore Hoyt, Eleazer Hudson, *Nathaniel Hunt, *Phillip Hunt, Phillip Hunt, Robert Jenkins, Ezekial Jewett, Thomas Jewitt, John Jones, *William Jones, Thomas Kimbal, William Kimball, David Knight, John Lakeman, Thomas Loney, Stephen Lowater, *Stephen Lowwater, Joseph Machem, George Mace, William Mansfield, Samuel Marshall, *Josiah Martin, Elijah Maxwell, Jacob Merrell, William Mitchell, *Jacob Morril, Andrew Morse, *Edmund Morse, Joseph Nicholes, *William Noyce, Jonathan Page, *Jonathan Page,

FREEMEN, FREEHOLDERS, AND CITIZEN SOLDIERS 77

Nathan Patch, William Pell, Michael Phetlock, Mich. Philbrook, John Philips, Thomas Pike Jr., Francis Poland, John Presby, John Preson, Moses Pressey, Eli Prichard, Jeffry Pulver, *Moses Pussey, James Reynolds, Stephen Richardson, David Rigges, David Riggs, *Andrew Roahdey, *Abra Safford, Jeremiah Seachell, Edward Seakes, William Semons, James Serjeant, Samuel Serjant, Thomas Serjant, Treworthy Serjant, John Small, Jacob Smith, Samuel Smith, William Smith, Jonathan Spain, James Stephens, Nicholas Stevens, Thomas Stowlet, Jonathan Swain, Samuel Thompson, John Tolinsbury, Zachary Trafton, Jacob Truck, James Turner, Samuel Tutle, Samuel Tuttle, Elemaleck Weid, Serjent Weide, Ebenezer Wheeler, Peter Wheeller, Ebenezer Whiph, William Whitwell, Simeon Williams, *Daniel Willit, Thomas Wing, Sippie Wood, Andrew Woodbury, Isaac Woodbury, *Stephen Woodward, Gideon Woodwell, Abram Young

1756
Ft. William Henry, Ft. Edward

Col. Jonathan Bagley

Lt. Col. John Kingsbury

Major Bensley Glazier, Stephen Miller

Capt. Nathaniel Blake, Stephen Blake, Israel Davis, Samuel George, Thomas Hartwell, Timothy Houghton, Hesekiel Hutchins, Joseph Ingersoll, Stephen Sargent, ---- Tapley, John Taplin, George Warthin, Stephen Webster, Gideon Woodwell, Benaiah Young

Lt. James Andrews, John Bagley, Benjamin Bridge, Ebenezer Brown, Timothy Colby, Ebenezer Cox, Josiah Fay, Jonathan Fessenden, Samuel George, Samuel Greenleaf, Hezekiah Hutchins, Nathaniel Ingersoll, Benjamin Kingsberry, John Kingsberry, Samuel Long, Thomas Stevens, Daniel Tucker, John Whitcomb, Gideon Woodwell

Ens. Timothy Colby, William Cox, Elisha Cummings, Abraham Gale, Edward Glover, Jonathan Hidden, Elijah Houghton, Stephen Ilsley, Jonathan Keny, Moses Prince, Josiah Sergant, Gilbert Thornton, Daniel Wheelwright, Samuel Williams

Adj. Morrill Whicher (Witcher), Adj. John Whiteing, Armorer Peter Johnson, Armorer David Blasdell, Armorer's Asst. Isaac Blasdell, Chpl. John Wood, Clk. Samuel Bachelder, Clk. John Bush, Clk. Jonas Cutler, Clk. Abijah Hall, Clk. Jonathan Johnson, Clk. John Lowell, Clk. John Loyd, Clk. Bradley Morison, Clk. Thomas Parsons, Clk. Joseph Remick, Clk. William Whitcomb, Comm. William Taylor, Comm. Moses Emerson, Secrt. Henry Liddel, Surg. Amos Putnam, Surg Mate James Otis, Surg Mate Benjamin Gavitt, Q.M. Joseph Remick

Sgt. John Abbott, Levi Andrews, Humphrey Atkins, Joseph Baker, Richard Barnes, Samuel Blackinbury, Daniel Blake, James Carr, Gideon Challis, Stephen Clark, William Conners, John Currier, Amos Davis, James Gross, Justinian Holden, Francis Hollady, James Mars, Moses Marsh, Benjamin Parker, Richard Peabody, Anthony Potter, Joseph Rose, Henry Stone, Daniel Sulivy, Uriah Tucker, Lemuel Vose, John Witcomb, Jonas Wilder, Joseph Worthen, George Worthy

Corp. Thomas Alexander, Jonathan Allen, James Bailey, Jonas Ball, William Barker, Nathan Barrett, John Barrill, Nathaniel Bishop, Joseph Bovery, John Buller, Benjamin Darnell, Thomas Dascom, Abel Davis, Ebenezer Davis, Peter Engenfield, Benjamin Estey, Henry Evans, Andrew Floyd, Ezekiel Foster, Jacob French, James Hair, John Hancock, Stephen Haskell, Nathaniel Hudson, Peter Johnson, Samuel Kinney, Ezekiel Lewitt, Gideon Lowell, Moses Lowell, Hezekiah Miller, Jonathan Norton, Jonathan Noyes, John Peirce, Jonathan Pierce, Isaac Remick, Daniel Samson, Thaddeus Spring, Nicholas Stevens, William Stockman, Gideon Straw, Thomas Thompson, Peter Wheeler, Jonas Whitney, Elisha Woodbury

Drum. Joseph Adams, Daniel Amos, Ephraim Boynton, John Carter, Hezekiah Dwinnell, Aaron Mason, Charles Sergeant, Philip Sergeant

Centinel Joseph Abrahams, Aaron Adams, Adellington, James Alger, Isaac Allard, John Astings, John Atkinson, Joseph Atkinson, Reuben Austen, Nathaniel Badcock, Benjamin Bagley, Charles Bagley, Abner Bailey, Kiah Bailey, William Baldwin, William H. Ballard, Abraham Barnes, Benjamin Barrett, Edward Barwick, James Bayley, Edward Bean, James Bean, Moses Bedunah, Jonathan Belden, Anthony Bell, Jonathan Bellows, William Benjamin, Joshua Betill, Jonathan Bigelow, Jonathan Bishop, Peter Black, Peter Blackmore, Isaac Blafoat, Jacob Blaisdell, Moses Blaisdell, Abiel Blake, Timothy Blake, Joseph Blancherd, William Bond, James Bowing, Thomas Boyden, Samuel Boyers, Saunders Bradbury, Wymond Bradbury, Samuel Bradstreet, John Broadstreet, Abejah Brown, Asa Brown, Ebenezer

FREEMEN, FREEHOLDERS, AND CITIZEN SOLDIERS

Brown, John Brown, William Brown, Abram Bruce, Ebenezer Buck, John Buck, Gershom Burbank, Sias Burbank, Joseph Burnam, Simons Bussell, William Caleb, Ezekiel Carr, George Carr, Josiah Carr, Sanders Carr, John Carter, John Casety, Philemon Casety, Daniel Casey, John Castling, Edward Castlow, Samuel Cathow, Cornelius Cavanaugh, Samuel Chadwell, Joseph Chamberlin, Phillips Chandler, Daniel Chapman, Phillip Chase, William Clerk, Joseph Clough, John Coffin, William Coffin, Joseph Coker, Adonijah Colby, Ezekiel Colby, Hezekiah Colby, Joshua Colby, Abijah Cole, Ebenezer Collins, William Colton, John Connell, Patrick Conner, John Cooper, William Cosewell, Benjamin Cox, Samuel Creasy, Ebenezer Crowfoot, Caesar Cuntea, Nicholas Currier, William Currin, James Curruth, Daniel Curtis, Jonathan Daniels, Reuben Darnell, Abel Davis, Michael Davis, Isaac Day, James Dayley, John Deane, Patrick Disney, John Dogget, Seth Dogget, Richard Dole, James Dow, Peter Dow, David Downing, John Downing, Joseph Downing, Thomas Dulles, Josiah Dunn, Samuel Eady, Soloman Eager, Thomas Eliot, Edmund Emery, Joseph English, Simeon Evans, Joseph Evelith, Ebenezer Fellock, William Fenick, Joshua Fisher, Timothy Fisher, Daniel Fisk, David Fisk, Thomas Fisk, Elisha Flag, Enoch Flag, Joseph Flander, Lewis Flander, Enoch Flanders, Nehemiah Flanders, Morris Fling, John Foot, Thomas Ford, Abner Foster, Jonathan Foster, Mark Fraizer, Joseph Freeman, Solomon French, Timothy French, Silas Frost, Josiah Fuller, Joseph Garling, Hezekiah Gates, Oliver Gates, David Gay, Jeremiah Gay, Gideon George, Samuel George, Ezra Getchill, Daniel Giddens, George Gieer, Zachariah Glazer, Isaac Gleeson, Joseph Godfrey, Benjamin Gold, John Gold, Jacob Goldthwait, Michael Goldthwait, Benjamin Goodale, John Goodridge, Enoch Goodwin, Samuel Gookin, Peter Goss, Noah Gould, Samuel Greenleaf, Ebenezer Greeno, Jonathan Griffin, James Hackit, John Hackit, Theophilus Hackit, Gershom Hale, Abijah Hall, Marmaduke J. Hamilton, William Harding, Joshua Hardy, Thomas Harrington, Matthias Hartman, John Hartshorne, Joseph Hartwell, Solomon Hartwell, John Harvey, Theophilus Harvey, Andrew Hasting, Samuel Haws, Stephen Haws, Jonathan Heath, William Hewins, Benjamin Hide, Abraham Hill, Asa Holegate, Edward Holland, Christopher Holmes, Zebulon Holmes, Uriah Holt, David Horton, Edmund Horton, Joseph Hovey, Thomas Hovey, Isaac How, Timothy Howard, Theodore Hoyt, Peter Hubbard, William Hubbard, Darius Hudson, Eliezer Hudson, Abijah Humphrey, Ezekiel Hunt, Moses Hunt, Nathaniel Hunt, William Hunt, Zebedee Hunt, Benjamin Hutchins, John Hutchins, David Ireland, Paul Isley, Dillington Johnson, Hezekiah Johnson, Moses Johnson, Nehemiah Johnson, Jacob Jones, Samuel Jones, Thomas Jones, Elijah Jordan, Samuel Jordan, Thomas Jordan, Timothy Kemp, James Kendrick, Nathaniel Kenney, Jonathan Kenny, Daniel Kent,

Richard Kent, Jacob Kibler, David Kimball, Thomas Kimball, Asa Kimble, John Kinchin, Ebenezear Knap, Daniel Knight, David Lane, Jonathan Laurance, David Leonard, John Leviston, Jabez Lewis, Ebenezer Liscomb, John Liscomb, James Lisle, Thomas Loney, Robert Longley, Eliphalet Lowell, Jonathan Lowell, Jacob Ludwick, Bernard Mace, George Mace, Thomas Manning, Isaiah Martin, Silas Mathews, Joseph Maxfield, Obediah Maxfield, Hugh Maxwell, Joseph May, Alexander McCoy, Francis McFadden, Josiah McGoon, John McNab, James McNeal, William McNeal, Joshua Merrill, James Metoon, Richard Millendy, John Milliken, William Mitchell, Elijah Molton, Elijah Molton, Benjamin Moore, Francis Moors, Richard Morgan, Samuel Morgaridge, William Morgaridge, Edward Murphy, Ebenezer Nast, Ambrose Nelson, Samuel Nevers, Moses Newland, Joshua Newton, Richard Newton, Aaron Nicholas, William Nicholas, Samuel Nichols, Isaac Norcross, Jonathan Noyes, Nathaniel Noyes, William Nuross, Hezekiah Oben, Thomas Obrian, Samuel Osgood, Solomon Osgood, Josiah Pacist, Bartholomew Packer, Abraham Page, Nathan Page, Josiah Parker, Zachariah Parker, Samuel Payson, David Peabody, John Penny, Jacob Perkins, Benjamin Perley, Eliakim Perry, Josiah Perry, Israel Persey, Edward Pettingale, Joseph Pettingale, Matthew Pettingale, Ephraim Philbrooks, Moses Pilsberry, Elijah Pilsbury, Nathaniel Piper, Aaron Pixley, Joseph Pogonit, William Pool, Samuel Potter, Jonas Powers, John Presby, James Puffer, Pitt Punham, Asaph Putnam, Robert Rag, Ephraim Ramsdell, Hanniniah Ran, John Rand, Charles Realy, Elijah Reed, James Rennelds, Zerah Ricker, Daniel Riggs, Samuel Roads, John Robbins, John Robbins, Elijah Robinson, Oliver Robinson, Josiah Robison, Jonathan Rogers, Samuel Rogers, Richard Russell, Joseph Samson, Edward Sanders, Humphrey Sanders, Jeremiah Satchell, Benjamin Saunders, James Sawing, Benjamin Sawyer, Richard Sawyer, Zebediah Sergeant, Josiah Sessions, Moses Sever, Sumner Shackford, Daniel Shepard, John Shepard, John Sinkler, John Small, Ballard Smith, David Smith, Ebenezer Smith, Jacob Smith, John Smith, Joseph Smith, Seth Smith, Zebediah Smith, Josiah Spaulden, Benoni Spear, Ruggles Spooner, Thomas Spywood, Samuel Staples, George Start, Phineas Stearns, Solomon Stickney, Robert Stocker, Joseph Stockman, Samuel Stockwell, Joseph Streeter, Joseph Suliva, Jonathan Sulivay, Samuel Swan, Moses Sweet, Samuel Sweet, Amaziah Talbot, Daniel Talbot, Samuel Tapley, William Taunt, Edward Thomson, Francis Town, Richard Townsend, Joshua Train, Jacob Truck, Joseph Tucker, Simeon Tupper, Abner Turner, Daniel Tusk, Jabez Upham, Seth Vose, Nathaniel Walker, Samuel Wallingford, William Walter, Michael Ware, Jonathan Warren, Phineas Watkins, Pelatiah Watson, Jonathan Wayman, Samuel Webster, John Weed, Enoch Welk, Silas Wellman, Enoch Wells, Joseph

Wells, Phillip Wells, Samuel Wells, Sion Wentworth, Elias West, Joseph Weston, Peter Wheeler, William Wheeler, Green Whillier, Abel Whitcomb, Levi Whitcomb, Silas Whitcomb, Jonathan Whitmore, Josiah Whitney, Joseph Whitten, Joseph Whittington, Joseph Whittom, Daniel Willett, Ebenezer Williams, Thomas Willington, Barnabas Willson, Michael Wilson, Edmund Winget, Morrell Wisher, Richard Woodbury, John Woods, Martin Woolford, Oliver Worcester, Ezekiel Worthen, Jonathan Worthen, Abraham Young, Joshua Young, Isaac Zachery

1757
*Ft. William Henry, Ft. Edward,
Amsberry Alarm List Co.*

Col. Jonathan Bagley

Major Stephen Miller

Capt. William Baily, Jonathan Barnard, Israel Davis, Samuel George, Hezekiah Hutchins, Stephen Sargent, John Taplin, George Worthin

Lt. Benjamin Balch, Joseph Blake, Joel Bradford, James Carr, Ebenezer Cox, David Titcomb

Ens. William Barron, Timothy Colby, Abraham Gale, Joseph Greenleaf

Armorer David Blasdell, Armorer Isaac Blasdell, Armorer Peter Johnson, Cornet. Joseph Goodwin

1758
Lake George, Ft. Edward

Col. Jonathan Bagley

Lt. Col. John Wetcomb (Whitcomb)

Major Joseph Ingersoll

Capt. James Andrews, Israel Davis, Andrew Fuller, Samuel George, Andrew Giddinge (Giddings), Ebenezer Marrow, Edmund Mooers, Joseph

Newhall, John Taplin, Stephen Whippell (Whipple), Asa Whitcomb, Salmon Whitney

Lt. Nathaniel Baily, Nathan Brigham, Joseph Buck, Samuel Burditt, Nathan Burnam, Peter Carlton, Judah Clark, Thomas Colby, Archelous Fuller, Darius Green, Benjamin Hastings, Hezekial Hutchins, Israel Hutchinson, Joseph Ilsley, Nathaniel Ingersoll, Stephen Low, Isaac Martin, Jonathan Pearson, Richard Sykes, Francis Temple, Leonard Whiting (Whittney)

Ens. Samuel Bacon, William Bagley, Samuel Davis, Joseph Greenleaf, John Holt, Samuel Knowlton, Zachariah Longley, Isaac Lovejoy, Abiel Messer, Pearly (Parley) Pike, Daniel Porter, Thomas Trowbridge

Adj. Richard Sykes, Chpl. John Cleaveland, Comm. of the Muster Henry Leddel, Q.M. William Taylor, Surg. Caleb Rea, Surg. Ward Noyce, Surg. Mate Ward Noyce, Surg. Mate Alexander Thompson

Centinel Benjamin Atherton, Ibijah Boyenton, Joseph Boynton, Bullet, Timothy Colby, Josiah Danns, Joseph Jesuit, Joseph Keyes, Ebinezer Knight, I. Lousioye, Joshua Parker, Josiah Procter, Richard Robins, Thomas Moriam, Joshua Pearce, James Sanderson, J. Sawyer, David Spalford, Jonathan Sprague, E. Starns, Joseph Suckers, Oliver Timey, Samuel Tredwell, Josiah Ward, Levi Whitcomb, Robert Whitcomb, Jonathan Whitney, Richard Wier, David Woodman, Joseph Woods

1759
Louisbourg, Canada

Col. Jonathan Bagley

Lt. Col. William Arbuthnot

Major Joseph Goldthwait

Capt. Edward Blake, Humphry Chadburn, Israel Davis, Andrew Fuller, Samuel George, Andrew Giddinge (Gidding, Giddings), Samuel Glover, George Hanner, Edmund Mooers, Joseph Newall, John Taplin, Stephen Whippell, Asa Whitcomb

FREEMEN, FREEHOLDERS, AND CITIZEN SOLDIERS

Lt. John Baker, Humphry Bradstreet, Edmund Brown, Timothy Colby, Edward Emerson, Thomas Emerson, William Greenleaf, Benjamin Hastings, Waldo Henderson, Edward Hopkins, Benjamin Kimball, Samuel Knowlton, Isaac Martin, Michael Martin, Joshua Moody, Johnson Moulton, Enoch Poor, Samuel Reed, Francis Temple, Abraham Tuckerman, Isaac Tuckerman, Ames Williams

Ens. Timothy Barnard, Josiah Berry, John Burril, Timothy Colby, Elisha Hewes, Benjamin Ingalls, Zachariah Longley, John Lord, William McElroy, John Roundey, Dummer Sewall, William Taylor, Caleb Woodberry, Josiah Woodbury

Adj. John Edwards, **Chpl.** John Cleaveland, **Comm.** Edward Sheaff, **Drum.** John Baker, **Drum.** William Browne, **Drum.** Hesediah Ellwill, **Drum.** Jonah Hall, **Drum.** Benjamin Abbott, **Drum.** Thomas Handley, **Drum.** (?) Howard, **Drum.** William Hillery, **Drum.** John Mears, **Drum.** Jacob Merratt, **Drum.** Moses Merrell, **Drum.** David Tuttle, **Drum.** Jonathan W (?), **Surg.** John Calef, **Surg.** Caleb Rea, **Surg. Mate** John Berry, **Surg. Mate** Ward Noyes, **Surg. Mate** Samuel Rogers, **Q.M.** William Taylor

Sgt. Augustas Berry, William Bowman, James Burwell [sic], Benjamin Chase, John Clark, Joshua Collins, James Cooper, Edward Day, William Downing, William Eaton, James Elliot, Daniel Griffin, John Harvay, Abram Ingraham, Timothy Johnson, (?) Jones, Jacob Martin, John McComm, James McDonald, William Mugeridge [sic], John Philips, Henry Putnam, Joseph Putnam, Samuel Reddington, Robert Simmons, James Whitaken, William Simmons, Richard Smith, (?) Stephens, William St. Lawrance, Benjamin Tinder, Jacob Thompson, Benjamin Toupen, Benjamin Varny, William Wheeler, William Wise

Corp. Josiah Burgess, Samuel Carthy, John Chandler, Philbrook Coolby [sic], Joseph Dunnham, James Eastman, Caleb Emory, Joshua Edwards, Simon Frye, Abraham Galehal, Charles Garritt, Robert Giterrmor [sic], John Gould, Richard Grepcoch, Moses Grimes, George Harrison, Samuel Hashaw, Jacob Hoskins, Mathew Knapp, Elisha Lyncold, William Midleton, Philip Miller, Joseph Odell, Abram Page, Samuel Palingall, Daniel Parrot, Phinias Parsons, William Plumer, Elisha Richmond, Thomas Simmons, Richard Skidmore, Ebinezer Snow, Joseph Stites, Robert Sturditon, Rubin Woodwell

Centinel Nathan Abbott, Aron Adams, Joshua Allan, David Allen, Isaac Allen, John Allen, Elisha Andrass, Moses Archs, William Joseph Attelton,

Joseph B. Attwood, Ebinezer Babbell, Daniel Babbidge, Benjamin Bagley, William Baldwin, Jonathan Barney, Thomas Barns, Timothy Barnes, Joshua Benens, Thomas Bear, Jonathan Belcher, Daniel Bell, David Beverly, Joshua Bickford, Jonathan Biggsby, Abram Binscut, Mathew Bixby, Nicholas Blasdale, (?) Blasdale, Samuel Blasdale, David Blunt, John Bolton, Benjamin Bolwell [sic], Rolison Bond, Charles Bowen, (?) Bradford, Zacharriah Brooker, James Broshell, Josiah Brown, Benjamin Browne, Francis Browne, William Browne, Ebenezer Bruce, (?) Burnamore, Jonathan Butterfield, George C., Zack Cadwell [sic], George Caidge [sic], Hugh Caine, Nehemiah Campbell, Edward Canns, Henry Casgrain, David Carner, Francis Carr, John Carr, Samuel Carr, Calib Chase, Guidion Challis, Philip Chandler, William Chappen, John Child, George Clarke, William Clemons, John Clough, Josiah Clough, (?) Coffin, Joseph Connent, William Cooke, Samuel Coony, Aron Copy, Osgood Cotton, Nathaniel Covel, Richard Crebert [sic], William Cronney, Morris Currin, Jonathan Darling, Charles Daus, John Davilt, (?) Davis, Philip Delaware, John Delay, Francis Deluly, (?) Demery, John Depbiere [sic], Edward Dispaw, Joseph Dole, Benjamin Downing, David Downing, William Dridge [sic], Michael Drivert, Jacob Duchindorff [sic], Abram Dunant, John Dunham, Stephen Dyer, Edward Eaden, Thomas Eaden, Timothy Eaden, Ebinezer Eaton, Walter Edmond, Joseph Edwards, Andrew Elflam, Phinias Emes, John Emons, Benjamin Emory, Richard English, John Eveno, Daniel Evesson, John Farnhum, James Farres, Andrew Farrow, Jonathan Fast, Paul Faulkosen [sic], David Fime, George Fish, George Fisk, Isaac Fisk, John Fisk, William Fitzgarald, Thomas Flack, Isaac Follett, Malachi Fost, Benjamin Foster, Joseph Fowle, Benjamin Fowles, George Frank, Mark Fraser, Mathew Freeman, James French, Joshua French, Moses French, Sampson French, Benjamin Frye, Joshua Fuller, Joshua Fulton, John Garland, John Gatt, John Gilbrist, Jonathan Gilbrist, James Giles, John Gillison, John Godfray, Michael Godwin, William Gosslford [sic], John Goldthouget [sic], John Good, John Goodridge, Thomas Gorden, Martin Graset, Daniel Gray, Ephrum Gray, John Gray, John Gray Junior, Joshua Gray, Daniel Greenleaf, Andrew Griffin, Mathew Griffin, William Griggins, John Grimes, Charles Grits, George Hadley, James Hadley, Joshua Hadley, Daniel Hagger, Amos Hall, John Hall, Stephen Hall, Edward Hammon, Richard Hammon, Jacob Harnot, Samuel Harver, Guilford Hathaway, Joshua Heath, Edward Herron, Niehemiah Herron, Benjamin Hodgdan, Seamon Hodgdan, (?) Hodgekins, James Holmon, Samuel Holt, Jacob Holton, John Holton, Thomas Howard, Jacob Hoyt, Samuel Hoyt, William Hoyt, Abram Hubert, John Hubert, Benjamin Huchins, Joseph Huchings, Abram Hicks, Levi Hooper, Samuel Hughes, Amos Hulton, Samuel Hulton, Edward Hunt, Joseph Hutchins,

William Hutchins, George Hutchinson, Jonathan Iewett, Abijah Ingalls, Joseph Jackson, Mathew Jesling [sic], Edward Kimball, Ebenezer King, Elisha King, Theodore King, Philip Klyne, Thomas Knorelton, Moses L., Elison Lasel, Stephen Lager, Robert Lash, Robert Laskey, Joseph Lauramey, John Lawrance, John Leatherby, Joseph Leatherby, Samuel Lebby, Nehemiah Lee, Edward Long, Benjamin Longly, James Lord, William Louse, Richard Luscombe, Oliver Lyncoln, Jonathan Lynday, Jebadia Lyneafor [sic], Mangarson, William Mansfield, Anthony Marshall, William McFirson [sic], Michael Lynch, Daniel McClaray, (?) McDonald, John McNeale, Daniel Means, Jacob Merrell, John Merrell, Isaac Mitchin, David Miller, George Miller, Mathew Milwook, Jonathan Mitchell, Joseph Moffitt, Samuel Morrison, David Morse, Elisha Morse, Isaac Morse, David Moullon, Philip Muntusk, Thomas Murphy, David Nemens, Richard Newhall, Samuel Noyes, Joseph Ofelaway [sic], David Oheron, John Oleman, Philip Ormond, John Orr, Oliver Osgood, Hezekial Owen, Michael Page, William Page, Joshua Pagnett, Jonathan Parker, Jonathan Parsons, John Paul, Asha Phimes, Joshua Pichman, (?) Pike, William Perry, Robert Piekoll, Timothy Pilbury, Benjamin Pool, Joseph Prainger [sic], (?) Pratt, Eleory Pratt [sic], Jonathan Prockter, Enoch Randker, David Randle, William Ray, George Read, Isaac Reed, Binson Richardson, David Richardson, Thomas Richardson, Winston Richardson, John Rigatt [sic], Dennis Ripters, Jonathan Rhoades, John Rogers, Stephen Rogers, Henry Ryons, James Seamons, Numan Searleth, John Shapose, Catto Sharp, Daniel Shaw, John Shaw, John Shordwont [sic], Benjamin Johnson, Joshua Kent, Samuel Kendrick, Henry Ketler, William Ketler, Mathew Kern, Inow Kern, Mathew Kidaale [sic], John Kiltson, Richard Shortwell, William Shraggue, Abram Smith, Arron Smith, David Smith, Henry Smith, Hesakia Smith, Jonathan Smith, John Smith, Solomon Smith, Solomon Smith, Walter Smith, David Snowford, William Snowtial, Hiah Spanders [sic], Jonis Spanders [sic], Elisha Spring, Carl Spooner, Jonathan Stanwood, Ebenezer Staple, Church Stardifne [sic], Isaac Stardifnt, Daniel Stayden, Jonathan Steele, William Stephans, Samuel Stickney, James Stinson, Bernard Stites [sic], John Stofer, Robert Stoker, John Stone, Josiah Stone, Robert Stone, Robert Sutton, John Syden, John Henry Sydar, Samuel Taylor, Seaman Taylor, Elisha Tenca, Timothy Thompson, Moses Thorp, David Timothy, William Tinglers, Seth Togg, Mathew Tolin, Thomas Toss, John Townsend, William Townsend, Esekial Transier, Jacob Trask, Francis Trebue, William Trought, Bradbury True, Daniel Tubbs, Josiah Turrell, Andrew Toothaker, Samuel Tuck, John Tucker, John Tuttle, Samuel Tuttle, Henry Tuxburry, Leth Twiney, John Twist, Joseph Varny, John W., Ichabod Wade, Samuel Wade, Moses Wadley, Benjamin Waistcoate, Thomas Waistcoate, Benjamin Wakefield, Niles Wale,

FREEMEN, FREEHOLDERS, AND CITIZEN SOLDIERS

Benjamin Walker, William Walker, Jacob Wallis, Nicholas Ward, John Warner, Nehemiah Wells, Jason West, Silas Westworth [sic], Jonathan Wheeler, Josh Wheelright, Hayfield White, Amos Whitting, John Wibbor, Solomon Withenell, Henry Willabor, Joshua Willabor, Andrew Willes, William White, Nathaniel Whitney, Ebenezer Williams, Elhaniah Williams [sic], Jonathan Williams, Joseph Williams, Silas Williams, Isaac Winston, Mathew Wintworth, Moses Woodman, John Wool, John Woten, Jonathan Wright, Nathan Wright, Gideon Young

Followers Elizabeth Allen, Mary Bowen, Arleen Chandler, Jane Chapman, Abigail Davis, Nancy Goodman, Ann Griffin, Catherine Herron, Margaret Lynch, Mary McClair, Abigail McCoye, Margaret McFirson, Margaret Shortwell, Mary Spanders, Margaret Sutton, Ann Thornton, Etisha Timothy, Margaret Thompson, Rebecca Thompson, Hanah Trebue, Mary Trebue, Lourana Tubbs, Mary Wibb

1760
Louisbourg

Col. Jonathan Bagley

Lt. Col. William Arbuthnot

Major Joseph Goldthwait

Capt. Edward Blake, Israel Davis, Samuel George, Andrew Giddings, Samuel Glover, Hanners, Joshua Moody, Edmund Mooers, Joseph Newhall, Stephen Whipple

Lt. John Baker, Humphrey Bradstreet, John Burrill, Thomas Emerson, William Greenleaf, Waldo Henderson, Edward Hopkins, Samuel Knowlton, Isaac Martin, Michael Martin, Enoch Poor, William Taylor, Abraham Tuckerman, Isaac Tuckerman

Ens. Timothy Barnard, Josiah Berry, Timothy Colby, Elisha Hewes, Benjamin Ingalls, Alexander Mcleod, William M'cleroy, William McElroy, William Taylor

Adj. John Edwards, Chpl. Jonathan Townsend, Comm. Mate Edward Sheaffe, Surg. John Calef, Surg. Mate Ward Noyce, Surg. Mate Walles Rust

1761
Louisbourg, Canada

<u>Col.</u> Jonathan Bagley

<u>Major</u> Joseph Goldthwait

<u>Capt.</u> John Baker, Edward Blake, Israel Davis, Samuel George, Andrew Giddings, Samuel Glover, Joshua Moody, Edmund Mooers, Joseph Newhall, Francis Peabody

<u>Lt.</u> John Baker, Nathan Baker, Thomas Emerson, William Greenleaf, Waldo Henderson, Edward Hopkins, Samuel Knowlton, Isaac Martin, Michael Martin, Enoch Poor, William Taylor, Abraham Tuckerman, Isaac Tuckerman, Jacob Tyler

<u>Ens.</u> Josiah Berry, Benjamin Ingalls, William McElroy, Alexander Mcleod, William M'cleroy

<u>Adj.</u> John Edwards, <u>Surg.</u> John Calef, <u>Surg. Mate</u> Ward Noyce, <u>Q.M.</u> William Taylor

1762
Louisbourg

<u>Col.</u> Jonathan Bagley

<u>Lt. Col.</u> Andrew Cole

<u>Capt.</u> Edmund Mooers

Appendix 7:

JONATHAN BAGLY ORDERLY BOOK, 1758

American Antiquarian Society, Worcester, Mass.

Transcribed by:

Brenton C. Kemmer
B.S.E.D., M.A.

This transcription of the Jonathan Bagley Orderly Book is written with the spelling and grammatical errors intact as in the original.

The original Orderly Book contains 34 pages, counting the blank back page.

This Orderly Book has no cover except the front and final page. It measures approximately 7 by 5 inches.

The original is in the Orderly Book Collection of the American Antiquarian Society of Worcester, Massachusetts, and is published here by permission of the American Antiquarian Society.

Special Thanks must go to the American Antiquarian Society and Thomas Knowles for their help in this transcription.

The first two pages of the Orderly Book are unreadable. They seem to appear to be mixed with information, figures, and graffiti. The last inside page also has unreadable figures, names and graffiti.

Camp at Lake George August 20
Parole Kingsall
   Field officers for the piquatts this night Major Beckwaths Major Griswold & General Haverland shall to sett tomorrow morning at 9 of Clock at the Presedents tents who are to try all Prisionors who may be brought before them Coll Haverland Prisedant   5 Capt 5 Subs from the Regulors 1 Capt 1 Subs from the light Infantry Members Capt Reathinfords of the first Battalion is appointed to act as Debuty Judge advocate the Prisioners & Evidences names are to be sent to help this Night

Lake George August 21 1758
Regemental orders 1 Sub 1 Sergt & 10 men to be Detacht out of each Company and be ready at 8 Clock and put under the care of Capt Moor and to be employ in finishing the hospitle & bulding a gard house in the frunt of Regiment
                              Jonathan Bagly Coll

Camp at Lake George August 21 1758
Parole Louisburge
   For the day tomorrow Coll Grant & Whiteing Field officers for the piquatts This night Major West & Major Gage   The tents of the whole army to be struckt at least once a week and the ground ear'd when the weather is good The following Regiments to Recive provision tomorrow For 4 days Gennerall at 6 Coll Whiteing at 7 Coll Woster at 8 Coll Nickols at 9 Hart at 10 Rangers at 11 Partrige at 2 in afternoon Bagly at 3 Williams at 4 & Pribble at 5

Camp at Lake George August (22?)
Parole Boston

Field officers for the Piquatt this night Leut Coll Mersy Major Titcomb and 100 men from the line to be out daly to make Cartriges Thay are at the artilery Encampment at 6 Clock in the morning and follow Capt Auards Directions___

The sick & invilints of the sevrall Regt according the list in the hands of the agiatents to be imediately sent to Fort Edward with the Returned team___A carfull Sergt from the Regt to be sent to take care of them Thay are to carry with them a proporsion of tents and a month subsistance wich is to be Dlivered to Ensigne Herrin of the 42 Regt Who will see that every man has Daly a preporsion of Roots and Greens and that each of them Recive Daly 1 Gill of vinegar from the Commesary wich the men are to pay for.

Camp at Lake George August 23 1758
Parole Hallifax

For the day tomorrow Coll Haldemond Coll Woster Field officers for the piquatts this night Major Beckwith Leut Coll Payson Brigade Major Money Penney___Wm Moors John Andrews John Husstin and Thos Vinsent of Coll Gages Regt Light Infantry tryed at the Laft General Cort Marshall of wich Coll Haveland was presedent for Desartion Twas found guilty and sentenced Death Major General Abboy Cramby approves of the above sentance___And Leut Dunlap of the Ineskilling tryed at the above Cort marshall For mutiny and Insolent behaver to Leut Otten was found gilty of Insolent behaver and sentencd to rec 500 Lashes Major General Cromy approves of the above sentances

The Guard to be Releved tomorrow morning by the provencials Left wing monthly Return to be given in tomorrow

Camp Lake George August 24 1758

A Regimental Cort martial to sett this morning at the president tent to try all parsons that may be brought before them Capt Fuller president Leut Burk of Capt Moor Leut Eleslie Ensigne Lovejoy Ensigne Missen

Lake George August 24 1758

Parole New York

Field officers for the piquatts this night Major West Leut Coll Whitcomb A party Consisting of 1 field officer 2 Capt 9 Subaltans 12 Sergt 12 Corpll & 300 men from the Regulors with a Leut Coll & Major 5 Capt 15 Subs 20 Sergt 20 corpll & 500 men from the provintials to march tomorrow morning at 7 Clock to Releve the Detachment at the half Way Brook field officers for the Detachment Leut Coll Mersy Leut Coll Whord & Major Day____The Regulor Regt are to practise Marching and Forming and in the woods all forming and changing in colloms of Diferant Debth____The Proencials Regt to be out colectively 3 times a week to make themselves experts in marching and forming in the woods

Lake George August 25 1758

Parole Brunswik

For the Day tomorrow Coll Havurland Coll Williams Field officers for the piquetts This night Major Beckwith Leut Coll Hurgader Major Spittle____The Regt give in a

Return of there arms tomorrow morning spacifying there N.O. and who is wanting to compleat there present astablishment rank and File accounting for there Defishansee Returns to be given in by every Regt at 6 this evening to the brigade Major of the men who have be instructed in the servis of artillery____persuant to the sentance of the Cort martials of which Coll Haverland was presedent Joshua Andrews John Harriss John Vinsent Wm Moor of his Majesteys Regt of lite Infantry to suffer Death tomorrow morning at 9 Clock for Desution In the frunt of there one Regt and piquatt of that Regt to guard the above Prisinors from the provost and the hole Regt to be under arms to attend the esecution____The following Regt to Recive provision for 21 Day Coll Pribble at 5 Wm at 6 Bagly 7 Partrige 8 Rogers 9 Hart 10 Nicholls 11 Woster 2 Whighting 3 Lymond 4

    Regemental orders all the tents in the Regt to be struct tomorrow in morning at 9 Clock and Ensigne Godard wich will be shone them by the Quarter master 10 men to be Detachment of each company from Day to Day to cutt bark for themselves to lay on this order is to be a punctualy obey

                                  Jonathan Bagly Coll

                    Camp at Lake George August 27 1758
Parole Jursey
    For the Day tomorrow Coll Grant & Coll Prebble Field officers for the piquatt this night Major West Major Slapp Brigade Major Money Penney

Camp at Lake George August 28 1758
Parole Louisburgh
Field officers for the piquatt this night Major Beckwith & Major Gribwattlde____ The troops to fire a rejoycing Fire this evening for the sucksess of his Majestis arms in taking Lewisbough the Regements to be under arms and line the brest work at 6 Clock The Fireing to begin with 21 guns from the Royal Artillary and then from the Right of the 42 Regt Round the line and to Finish with the left of Coll Baglys Regt This to be Repeeted till the hole has Fired 3 Rounds____ The piquatts & gards not to Fire but to be formed in the Rere of there Regt The Commanding officers of Regts to order a reviue of them armed at 12 Clock and the Bawls to be drawn and have cartrige without Bawl to be made up For there Rejoyceing Fire

Lake George August 29 1758
Parole Parline
For the day tomorrow Coll Haldemon Coll Bagly Field officers this night Leut Eayrs Major Gage Major Rogers Rangers to Discharge there pesses this Eveing between 4 & 6 Clock The Connicut Regt with new Hamshiar Regt to do the duty of all the proencials troop tomorrow and the massachusetts Regt to be Musterd on Thursday by Major Stoton Brigade Major of the proventials begining with Coll Pribble at 7 Clock Coll Wm 10 Coll Bagly at 11 Coll Nickolls 21 afternoon____Doctor Munrow to Examin the Mediason Chest of every Regt Regulor and provential tomorrow afternoon and to Report to the General the Condition tha are in____ The Role to be called and if any man is misfing a Report to be made to the Brigade Major This eveing The following Regt to Recive 4 Day Provision General Lymond at 5 Coll Whiteing at 6 Coll Woster at 7 Coll Nikolls at 8 Coll Hart at 9 the Rangers at

10 Coll Partrig at 11 Coll Bagly at 12 Coll Williams at 2 afternoon

Lake George August 29 1758

Regimental orders, all the tents in the Rank in each company to be struck amediatly and ground well cleand where the tents stud and not be picht againe for 3 ours and then to pich on the same ground

Jonathan Bagly Coll

Lake George August 30 1758

Parole London
  Field officers For the piquatts Major West Major Spencer The Albony post to sett out this Evining

Camp at Lake George August 31 1758
Parole Doublon, ____ Field for the Day tomorrow Coll Haviland Coll Whiteing field officers for the piquatt this night Major Beckwith Major Tickomb Brigade Major Money Penney____ 1 Capt 1 Sub 2 Sergt 2 Corpoll and 40 men from the Rugolors with 1 Sub 1 Sergt 1 Corpoll & 20 men from the Rangers to hold them selves in Rediness to Embark on board the sloop tomorrow 100 men from the line to perrade at 2 Clock with out arms Tha are to go up to the woods and each of them bring in a load of brush to Cover the provitions

Lake George Septer 1 1758

Parole Hallafax

    Field officers for the piquatts this night Leut Coll Eayrs Leut Coll Payson____A Detachment of 4 Subs and 100 Volunteers from the Rangers the 3 company of light Infantry 100 of Major Rogers Rangers 100 of Coll Partrige Rangers 100 of Connutticuts Rangers to march tomorrow morning at 7 Clock with 7 Days Provision and in the command of Capt Dolyselle of the light Infantry Thay are to take the Convoy under there Escort to the half way brook There Detachment to be under arms this evening at 4 Clock on the ground near Where the old Fort stood When any prisionere or Deserters coms into camp the centy of guard that has them in charge is to conduct them Directly to head quarters and not suffer any person what so ever to ask them questians and no officer to stop or offer to ask questions of any Desorter or Prisoner on pane of Disobaying orders.

Lake George Sept 2 1758

Regimentiual orders

    1 Capt 3 Subs 4 Sergt and 54 Privates to be Detachtd out of the Right and Peraded Diretly to gett stuff and compleat the guard house under the Diretion and order of Major Ingasulle and the same number of officers & privats to be peraded at 8 Clock in the morning from Day to Day untill the Guard house is well comleated Sundays Excepted

Jonathan Bagly Coll

Lake George Sept 2 1758

Parole Plymouth

    For the Day tomorrow Coll Grant Coll Woster Feild officers for the piquatts this night Major Coll West Leut Coll Whitcomb Brigade Major Spittle all partey on piquatt marching out of Camp are allways to carry there Blanketts and 1 Days provitons   This to be a standing order the Generall proposes to see the 27 Regiment under arms at 7 Clock on munday morning for 42 at 10 44 at 1 in afternoon to perform what thay have practtosd in consequenc of the 24 of August____The following Regt to Recive 4 Days Provition tomorrow Coll Prebble at 5 Clock Coll Willimans at 6 Coll Bagly at 7 Coll Partrige at 8 Rangers 9 Coll Hart at 10 Coll Nickolls at 11 Coll Woster at 12 Coll Whiteing at 2 afternoon Coll Lymond at 3

Lake George Sept 3 1758
Parole Bristole ____field officers for the piquatts this night Major Beckwith Leut Coll Coyet no hutts nor houses to be bult in the streept of the Regt nor incampments near the Brest work so as to inturupt the Communication These allredy bult to be puld down____The following Regt to Receve 4 Days provition tomorrow 4 Battallion at 5 the 55 at 6 46 at 7 44 at 8 42 at 9 27 at 10 Royalamericans at 11

Camp Lake George Sept 4 1758
Parole Cork
    For the Day tomorrow Coll Haldeman Coll Williams field officers for the Piquatt this night Coll Eayrs Major Berrey Brigade Major Money Penny The Generall Proposses to see the 55 Regt under arms half after 7 tomorrow morning the 4 Battalion at 10____The Ditch to be filled and the ones to Work to be Keept in repair as the Commanding officer will be answerable____The Coll of the day of the Regulors Viz. Coll Grant to go round the incampment to see all Hutts Demollish That any way Obstruckt the Communication of the Bres work

Lake George Sept 5 1758
Parole Limbrick
　　　Field officers for the piquatt this night Major Beckwith Major Ingasulle The piquatt on the Island to be Relev'd this Day at 1 Clock by 1 Capt 1 Sub 2 Sergt 2 Corpll and 36 men from the Regulors 2 Subs 2 Sergt 2 Corpll and 36 men from the proventials The men to be chosen and to be such as have accoutimaid Boats and under stand Rowing This party to Carry 2 Weeks Provition

Camp at Lake George Sept 6 1758
Parole Deerfield
　　　Field officers for the piquatt this night Leut Coll Eayrs Major Slap
　　　For the Day tomorrow Coll Hart Coll Haverland____ field officers for the piquatts This night Leut Coll Eayrs Major Slap on allarm in the night Regt of Coll Williams and Prebble and Bagly are to man the brest work from the hospitell on the Right of the Brest work on the flank of the Regulors amiriacans to the left of the Encampment of the 42 Regt leaving the Ground Where the firs battalion of Royall american Encampt to be occupied by Brigadear Gages light Infantry to wich tha occupied is to be left on alarm from the sally port on the right of the Royall amiricans Coll Partrige corps Major Rogers Rangers to com to the line of the Great Rode and to fall into the left of the 42 Regt Coll Harts Coll Wosters Genorall Lymonds Coll Nickoll Regt Coll Nickolls and Coll Whitings from thence to the Hospitell the Grannadear of the piquatt of the Regulors are to be a body of resarve and to assemble on any aleram be hind the work markt out for them in the rear of the 42 Regt the Piquatt of the 42 Regt to march Down to the Rode and take post at the Hospitell fort The

troops to be under arms at 7 Clock tomorrow morning and Each Corps to be formed at there Alarm Post the light Infantry and Rangers to com into the line at the same time____ the commisery to Deliver out fish for ration to the Regt accorden to there number and the Commanding officer to Devide of Regt to the sick___

The following Regt to recive provition for 21 Days General Lymond at 5 Coll Whiteing at 6 Coll Woster at 7 Coll Nickolls at 8 Coll Hart at 9 the Rangers at 10 Coll Partrage at 11 Coll Bagly at 12 Coll Wm at 2 Coll Prebble at 3

Camp at Lake George Sept 7 1758
Parole Springfield
    Field officers for the piquatt this night Major Gage Major Beckwith the Coll of the Day to the Battoos and works and make a report of them and a Sergt & Corpll with 12 men from General Lymond Regt Coll Nickolls Regt to mount as a guard near the swamp in the Woods between the Regts and Incampment and to continue there till further orders The party at the halfway Brook is to be Relived tomorrow Morning by 1 coll 3 Capt 9 subs 12 Sergt 12 corpll and 300 men from the Regolors 1 leut coll 1 Major 5 Capt 15 subs 20 sergt 20 Corpll and 500 men from the provins The above party to perade at 7 clock and to Escort the Wagons from hence Coll Haverlan leut Coll Parssone and Major Gorswood for the above party The following Regt to Recieve 4 Day Provision tomorrow The Royall artillary at 5 clock 27 at 6 42 at 7 44 at 8 46 at 9 55 at 10 4 Battalion at 11 Light Infantry at 12

Lake George Sept 8 1758
Parole Westfield
    For the day tomorrow Coll Halderman Coll Nickolls field officers for the piquatt This night Major Misnster Major Spencer___orderly time for the muster to be at 5 clock in the evening

Lake George Sept 9 1758
Parole Catteroguy
    Field officers for the piquatt this night leut Coll Messay Major Titcomb__ all the tools in posesition of the several Regt to be Delivered to the Commisary tomorrow morning, The Regulors from 6 to 8 the provincials from 8 to 10 Proportion of tools will be Delivered to the Regt tomorrow afternoon

Camp at Lake George Sept 10 1758
Parole Boston
    For the Day tomorrow Grant Coll Lymond field officers for the piquatt this night, Major Beck with leut Coll Whitcomb Brigade Major Spittle___all persons going with passes and to sett out and keep the Escort non to be suffered to go before noon after it The advance guard to stop all persons Disobaying the order and to send them persons to head quarters all the post with out the camp to be very carefull that no people go beyond them and so check persons who attempt it___When a Escort is sent from any & have an officer from that & have to go to the above post by wich they are to pass and inform the commanding officer of it___The following Regt to recieve fresh provisions tomorrow for 2 Day Regt Coll Prebble at 5 clock Williams at 6 Coll Bagly at 7 Partrige at 8 Rangers at

9 Hart 10 Nickolls 11 Woster at 12 Wighting at 2 afternoon General Lymond at 3

Lake George Sept 11 1758

Parole London

Field officer for the piquatt this night leut coll Eayers leut Coll Coicle field officer of piquett to go the Round as all the army to be under arms half a ower after 4 this Evening the Regulors and light Infantry to be formed where the first Battalion of Royall americans where to camp the right Whing of the provincials where Coll Bagly incamped and the left wing and the Rangers in the front Lymond Regt to joyn the thanks giving in the taking catigoray after wich each corps is to form on there alarm post____ to join a Rejoyceing fire the fire to begin with 21 guns from the artillery and from the Right of the Inskilling Regt around the line and to finis with the left of Coll Bagly This to be repeated till the hole has fired 3 Rounds the piquatt and guard not to fire but to form in the Rear of there Regt____

The Commanding officer of Regt to order a Reve of Arms at 12 clock and the balls to be Drawn and cartrige to be used for there rejoceing fire____ each Regt may Receve from the Commasery of stores the Quarter master each 10 spads 5 fallen axes and pick axes no larger quantity of all will be allowed as there is no broad axes in the stores but most are wanted for the public service non can be spaired for the Regt

SELECT BIBLIOGRAPHY
Of Important Readings

Primary Materials:

"A Journal of an Expedition Against Canada by Moses Dorr, Ensign of Capt. Parker's Co., 1758." *New York History* 16 (1935) 452-64.

"Account of the Capture of Fort Frontenac by the Detachment Under the Command of Col. Bradstreet, Journal Lieut. Benjamin Bass, 1758." *New York History* 14 (1935) 449-52.

An Impartial Account of Liet. Col. Bradstreet's Expedition to Fort Frontenac, 1758. Toronto: Rous & Mann Limited [1940].

Anderson, Fred, to Brenton C. Kemmer, 1994, Miscellaneous notes on *Timothy Nichols diary, 1759*; *James Henderson diary, 1758-1759*; *Nathaniel Bang Orderly Book, 1759*; *Samuel Ward diary, 1759*; *John Leach diary, 1757-1758*, Author's Private Collections, Houghton Lake, Michigan.

Benjamin Glasier Diary, 1758-1760. Photocopy Essex Institute, Salem, Massachusetts, Author's Private Collections, Houghton Lake, Michigan.

Broadside by His Excellency William Shirley, Esq., Enlistment Orders and Qualifications, April 17, 1755, p. 1. Manuscript in Broadside Collections, Clements Library, University of Michigan, Ann Arbor, Michigan.

"Diary of Capt. Asa Foster of Andover, Massachusetts, 1758." *New England Historic Genealogical Register*, 54 (1900): 183-88.

"Diary of Sergeant John Burrell, 1759-1760." *New England Historic Genealogical Register* 59 (1905) 352-54.

"Diary of Nathaniel Knap of Newbury, 1758." Society of Colonial
Wars in the Commonwealth of Massachusetts (1895) 1-42.

Edna V. Moffett, ed. "The Diary of a Private on the Expedition to
Crown Point, James Hill, 1755." *New England Quarterly* 5 (1932)
602-18.

"Extracts From the Diary of Reverend Samuel Chandler, 1755." *New
England Historic Genealogical Register* 17 (1863) 346-54.

Fox, Chris, to Brenton C. Kemmer, 1991, *Phinehas Lyman Orderly
Book*, 1757, Author's Private Collections, Houghton Lake,
Michigan.

Frederic Kidder, ed. "Journals of Joseph Holt of Wilton, New
Hampshire, 1758." *New England Historic Genealogical Register*
10 (1856) 307-11.

John Cleaveland Papers. Essex Institute; Salem, MA: Essex Institute,
1974. Text-microfilm.

"Journal of Stephen Cross of Newbury-Port, 1756." Essex Institute,
Historical Collections 76 (1940) 14-42.

Kochan, James L. "Joseph Frye's Journal and Map of the Siege of
Fort William Henry, 1757." *The Fort Ticonderoga Museum
Bulletin* 15 #5 (1993) 338-361.

Olson, Jerry, to Brenton C. Kemmer, 1990, Militia Discipline, "The
Words of Command and Directions for Massachusetts Militia,
1733," Author's Private Collections, Houghton Lake, Michigan.

Olson, Jerry, to Brenton C. Kemmer, 1990, *Archelaus Fuller Journal,
1758*, Author's Private Collections, Houghton Lake, Michigan.

Olson, Jerry, to Brenton C. Kemmer, 1990, *Samuel Cobb Journal,
1758*, Author's Private Collections, Houghton Lake, Michigan.

"The Anonymous Journal." *The Fort Ticonderoga Museum Bulletin* 12 (1968) 291-97.

"The Moneypenney Orderly Book." *The Fort Ticonderoga Museum Bulletin* 12 (1966-1970) 328-357, 434-461.

Piper, William S., ed. *Diary and Journal of Seth Metcalf, 1755-1807.* Boston: The Historical Records Survey, 1939.

Tomlinson, Abraham. *The Military Journals of Two Private Soldiers, 1758-1775.* New York: Books for Libraries Press, 1970.

Secondary Materials:

Brooke, John L. *The Heart of the Commonwealth, Society and Political Culture in Worcester County, Massachusetts.* Amherst, MA: The University of Massachusetts Press, 1989.

Clark, Charles E. *The Eastern Frontier, The Settlement of Northern New England.* London: University Press of New England, 1983.

Dow, George F. *Every Day Life in the Massachusetts Bay Colony.* New York: Dover Publications, Inc., 1988.

Earle, Alice M. *Home Life in Colonial Days.* Stockbridge, MA: Berkshire House, Publishers, 1993.

Field, Edward. *The Colonial Tavern.* Providence, RI: Preston and Ronds, 1897; repr., Bowie, Maryland: Heritage Books, Inc., 1989.

Flexner, James T. *Mohawk Baronet, A Biography of Sir William Johnson.* Syracuse, NY: Syracuse University Press, 1979.

Galley, Jeffery. "Women and the British Army." *The Journal of the Forces of Montcalm and Wolfe* 6 #3 (July 1993) 11-12.

Gaustad, Edwin S. *A Religious History of America*. New York: Harper & Row, Publishers, 1974.

Guilday, John E. *Archaeological Investigation of Fort Ligonier*. Pittsburgh, PA: Annals of Carnegie Museum, 1970.

Hamilton, Edward P. *Fort Ticonderoga, Key to a Continent*. Ticonderoga, NY: Fort Ticonderoga, 1995, reprint from American Historical Society, 1964.

Hill, George C. *Gen. Israel Putnam, A Biography*. Boston: E.O. Libby and Co., 1858.

Houlding, J.A. *Fit For Service, The Training of the British Army*. Oxford: Clarendon Press, 1981.

Hudson, Winthrop S. *Religion in America*. New York: Charles Scribner's Sons, 1973.

Hutchinson, Thomas. *The History of the Colony of Massachusetts-Bay, From 1749-1774*. London: John Murray, 1778; repr. New York: Arno Press, 1972.

Jedrey, Christopher M. *The World of John Cleaveland*. New York: W.W. Norton & Co., 1979.

Moseley, Bruce M. "The Amherst Punch Bowl." *The Fort Ticonderoga Museum Bulletin* 15 #5 (1993) 392-401.

Pell, S.H.P. *Fort Ticonderoga, A Short History*. Ticonderoga, NY: Fort Ticonderoga Museum, 1987.

Rogers, Col. H.C.B. The British Army of the Eighteenth Century. New York: Hippocrene Books, Inc., 1977.

Spring, Ted. *Sketchbook 56, The Highlanders and Provincial Rangers*. St. Louis, Missouri: The Brandy Press, 1984.

Stott, Earl and Jean. *Exploring Rogers Island.* Fort Edward, NY: Published by the authors, 1986.

Sweet, William W. *Religion in Colonial America.* New York: Charles Scribner's Sons, 1942.

Zaboly, Gary S. "A Royal Artillery Officer With Amherst, 1759." *The Fort Ticonderoga Museum Bulletin* 15 #5 (1993) 362. Special note to painting of aerial rendition of Lake George-Hudson River forts and outposts.

Index Of Names, Places, And Subjects

----, Jonathan W 83
ABBOTT, Benjamin 83 John 78 Nathan 83
ABBOYCRAMBY, Maj Gen 92
ABERCROMBY, Gen 24
ABRAHAMS, Joseph 78
ADAMS, Aaron 78 Aron 83 George 76 Joseph 78 Nathaniel 76
ADELLINGTON, 78
ALBANY, New York 17 32 35
ALEXANDER, Thomas 78
ALGER, James 78
ALLAN, Elizabeth 86 James 76 Joshua, 83
ALLARD, Isaac 78
ALLEN, David 83 Isaac 83 John 83 Jonathan 78
AMESBURY Mass., 6-7 9-10 13 Trades 13
AMESBURY FERRY Mass., 6
AMOS, Daniel 78
ANDERSON, Fred 5-6
ANDRASS, Elisha 83
ANDREWS, James 72 77 81 John 92 Joshua 94 Levi 78
APPLETON, John 76
ARBURTHNOTT, William 72
ARBUTHNOT, William 71 82 86
ARCHS, Moses 83
ASTINGS, John 78
ATHERTON, Benjamin 82
ATKINS, Humphrey 78
ATKINSON, John 78 Joseph 78

ATTELTON, William Joseph 83
ATTWOOD, John 76 Joseph B 84
AUARD, Capt 92
AUSTEN, Reuben 78
BABB, William 76
BABBELL, Ebinezer 84
BABBIDGE, Daniel 84
BACHELDER, Samuel 78
BACON, Samuel 74 82
BADCOCK, Nathaniel 78
BADGER, John 76 Joseph 36
BAGLEY, Benjamin 78 84 Charles 78 Dorothy 6 Dorothy Harvey 6 John 72 77 Jonathan 1 3 5-7 9-10 13 15 17-19 21 23-25 32 35 38-39 47 51-52 59 71-72 75 77 81-82 86-87 Jonathan Becomes Col 7 Jonathan, Military Career of 6-7 Jonathan Personal History of 5-7 Orlando 6 William 74 82 Winthrop 76
BAGLEY BRIDGE, 41
BAGLEY'S REGIMENT, History of 1-5 17
BAGLY, Jonathan 91 94-96 98-102
BAILEY, Abner 78 James 78 Kiah 78
BAILY, Nathaniel 72 82 William 81
BAKER, John 72-73 75 83 86-87 Joseph 78 Nathan 73 87
BALCH, Benjamin 72 81
BALDWIN, William 78 84
BALL, Jonas 78

BALLARD, William H 78
BARKER, William 78
BARNARD, Jonathan 81 Timothy 74 83 86
BARNES, Abraham 78 Richard 78 Timothy 84
BARNEY, Jonathan 84
BARNS, Thomas 84
BARRETT, Benjamin 78 Nathan 78
BARRILL, John 78
BARRON, Jonathan 72 75 William 81
BARWICK, Edward 78
BATTERIES, Floating 51
BATTLE OF LAKE GEORGE 3 27 31-32 62
BATTLE OF TICONDEROGA 37
BAY COLONY, 15 25 31 49 59
BAYLEY, James 78
BAYONETS, 31 35-36
BEAN, Edward 78 James 78
BEAR, Thomas 84
BECKWATHS, Maj 91
BECKWITH, 100 Maj 92-93 95-96 98-99 101
BEDSACKS, 36
BEDUNAH, Moses 78
BELCHER, Jonathan 84
BELDEN, Jonathan 78
BELE, Anthony 76
BELL, Anthony 76 78 Daniel 84
BELLOWS, Jnathan 78
BENENS, Joshua 84
BENJAMIN, William 78
BERREY, Maj 98
BERRY, Augustas 83 John 83 Josiah 74 83 86-87
BETILL, Joshua 78
BEVERLY, David 84
BICKFORD, Joshua 84

BIGELOW, Jonathan 78
BIGGSBY, Jonathan 84
BILLETING, 17
BINSCUT, Abram 84
BISHOP, Ebenezer 76 Jonathan 78 Nathaniel 78
BIXBY, Mathew 84
BLACK, Peter 78
BLACKINBURY, Samuel 78
BLACKMORE, Peter 78
BLACKS, In Bagley's Regiment 10
BLAFOAT, Isaac 78
BLAISDELL, Jacob 78 Moses 78
BLAKE, Abiel 78 Capt 35 56 Daniel 78 Edward 72-74 82 86-87 Joseph 72 81 Nathaniel 71-74 77 Stephen 71 77 Timothy 78
BLANA, Jedediah 76
BLANCHERD, Joseph 78
BLANKETS, 27 33 35 37-39 48
BLASDALE, ---- 84 Nicholas 84 Samuel 84
BLASDELL, David 78 81 Isaac 78 81
BLUNT, David 84
BOATBUILDERS, 3
BOLLAN, Mr 31
BOLTON, John 84
BOLWELL, Benjamin 84
BOND, Rolison 84 William 78
BOOKS, 21 32-33 51-52 55
BOOLD, Nehemiah 37
BOSTON, Massachusetts 9-10 13 92 101
BOTTLES, Wooden 39
BOUNTIES, Enlistment 15
BOVERY, Joseph 78
BOWEN, Charles 84 Mary 86
BOWING, James 78
BOWMAN, William 83

BOXFORD, Massachusetts 9
BOYDEN, Thomas 78
BOYENTON, Ibijah 82
BOYERS, Samuel 78
BOYNTON, Ephraim 78 Joseph 82
BRADBURY, Saunders 78
  Wymond 78
BRADFORD, ---- 84 Joel 72 81
BRADSTREET, Humphrey 73 86
  Humphry 83 Samuel 78
BREECHES, 27 35-36 51-52 55
BRIDGE, Benjamin 72 77
BRIGHAM, Nathan 73 82
BRISTOLE, 98
BROADSTREET, John 78
BROOKER, Zacharriah 84
BROSHELL, James 84
BROWN, Abejah 78 Asa 78
  Ebenezer 72 77-79 Edmund 73
  83 John 79 Josiah 84 Samuel 76
  Stephen 76 Thomas 76 William
  79
BROWNE, Benjamin 84 Francis 84
  William 83-84
BRUCE, Abram 79 Ebenezer 84
BRUNSWIK, 93
BUCK, Ebenezer 76 79 John 79
  Joseph 73 82
BUCKLEY, Joseph 76
BULLER, John 78
BULLET, 82
BULLET BAGS, 27
BULLET POUCH, 36
BURBANK, Gershom 76 79 Israel
  76 Sias 79
BURDITT, Samuel 72 82
BURGESS, Josiah 83
BURK, John 75 Leut 93
BURNAM, Joseph 79 Nathan 72 82
BURNAMORE, ---- 84
BURRIL, John 74 83

BURRILL, John 73 86
BURT, James 76
BURWELL, James 83
BUSH, John 78
BUSH FIGHTING, 52
BUSSELL, Simons 79
BUSWELL, Joseph 76
BUTMAN, Thomas 76
BUTTERFIELD, Jonathan 84
C, George 84
CADWELL, Zack 84
CAIDGE, George 84
CAINE, Hugh 84
CALEB, William 79
CALEF, John 83 86-87
CAMPBELL, John 76
CAMP FOLLOWERS, 55-56 *See
  also:* Women Camp Followers
CAMPGELL, Nehemiah 84
CANNS, Edward 84
CAPS, 27 30 32 35 38 47-48
CARILLON (Ft. Ticonderoga), 3
CARLSON, R 13
CARLTON, Peter 73 82
CARNER, David 84
CARPENTERS, 3 13 51 62
CARR, Ezekiel 79 Francis 84
  George 79 James 72 78 81 John
  84 Josiah 79 Samuel 84 Sanders
  79
CARTER, John 78-79
CARTHY, Samuel 83
CARTRIDGE BOXES, 39 48
CASADAY, Charles 76
CASETY, John 79 Philemon 79
CASEY, Daniel 79
CASGRAIN, Henry 84
CASTLING, John 79
CASTLOW, Edward 79
CATHOW, Samuel 79
CATTEROGUY, 101

CAVANAUGH, Cornelius 79
CHADBURN, Humphry 82
CHADWELL, Samuel 79
CHALLIS, Gideon 78 Guidion 84
CHAMBERLIN, Joseph 79
CHAMPLAIN, Lake 17 -Lake George Corridor 32
CHANDLER, Arleen 86 John 83 Philip 84 Phillips 79
CHAPLAIN, 10 17-18 25 59
CHAPMAN, Daniel 79 Jane 86
CHAPPEN, William 84
CHASE, Benjamin 83 Calib 84 Phillip 79
CHEYNEY, Daniel 76
CHILD, John 84
CHUDBURN, Capt 56
CLARK, John 83 Judah 82 Juday 73 Stephen 78 Thomas 76
CLARKE, George 84
CLAY, Jonas 76
CLEAVELAND, John 24 54 59 82-83 Rev 54
CLEMONS, William 84
CLERK, William 79
CLOUGH, 3 62 Gibson 48 61 John 84 Joseph 79 Josiah 84
COFFIN, ---- 84 John 79 William 79
COICLE, Leut Coll 102
COKER, Joseph 79
COLBEY, Phillip 76 Timothy 76 Timothy Jr 76
COLBIE, Phillip 76 Timothy 76
COLBY, Adonijah 79 Ezekiel 79 Hezekiah 79 Joshua 79 Thomas 73 82 Timothy 72-73 75 77 81-83 86
COLE, Abijah 79 Andrew 71 87
COLEBY, Philip 76 Timothy 76
COLLINGS, Ebenezer 76
COLLINS, Ebenezer 79 Joshua 83
COLTON, William 79
CONNELL, John 79
CONNENT, Joseph 84
CONNER, Patrick 79
CONNERS, William 78
CONNUTTICUTS RANGERS, 97
COOKE, William 84
COOLBY, Philbrook 83
COONY, Samuel 84
COOPER, James 83 John 76 79 Joseph 76
COPY, Aron 84
CORK, 98
COSEWELL, William 79
COTTON, Osgood 84
COVEL, Nathaniel 84
COX, Benjamin 79 Ebenezer 72 77 81 William 73 77
COYET, Leut Coll 98
CREASY, Samuel 79
CREBERT, Richard 84
CROMY, Maj Gen 92
CRONNEY, William 84
CROSS, Moses 76
CROWFOOT, Ebenezer 79
CROWN-POINT, 15
CROWN POINT, 1 15
CUMBERLAND COUNTY, MAINE, Bagley Granted Land And Settled In 7
CUMMINGS, Elisha 73 77
CUNTEA, Caesar 79
CURRIER, 3 John 78 Nicholas 79 Timothy 6
CURRIN, Morris 84 William 79
CURRUTH, James 79
CURTIS, Daniel 79
CUTLER, Jonas 78
DALTON, Samuel 76
DANIELS, John 76 Jonathan 79

DANNS, Josiah 82
DARLING, Jonathan 84
DARNELL, Benjamin 78 Reuben 79
DASCOM, Thomas 78
DAUS, Charles 84
DAVILT, John 84
DAVIS, ---- 84 Abel 78-79 Abigail 86 Amos 78 Capt 56 Ebenezer 78 Edmund 76 Ezekiel 76 Increase 76 Israel 71-74 77 81-82 86-87 Michael 79 Moses 76 Samuel 74 82
DAVISE, Ebenezer 76
DAY, Aaron 76 Edward 83 Isaac 79 Maj 93
DAYLEY, James 79
DEANE, John 79
DEERFIELD, 99
DELAWARE, Philip 84
DELAY, John 84
DELULY, Francis 84
DEMERY, ---- 84
DEMOGRAPHICS, of Bagley's Regiment 7-13
DENNIS, John 76
DEPBIERE, John 84
DIESKAU, 62 Baron 1 3
DILL, Joseph 76
DISNEY, Patrick 79
DISOBEDIENCE, 6 59-61
DISPAW, Edward 84
DODGE, Antipas 76 Israel 76
DOGGET, John 79 Seth 79
DOLE, Joseph 84 Richard 79
DOLTEN, Samuel 76
DOLYSELLE, Capt 97
DONNES, Gideon 76
DOUBLON, 96
DOW, James 79 Peter 79
DOWNES, Andrew 76

DOWNING, Benjamin 84 David 79 84 John 79 Joseph 79 William 83
DRIDGE, William 84
DRIVERT, Michael 84
DRUMMERS, 9-10 17-18 56
DRUMS, 35 47
DUCHINDORFF, Jacob 84
DULLES, Thomas 79
DUNANT, Abram 84
DUNHAM, John 84
DUNLAP, Leut 92
DUNN, Josiah 79
DUNNHAM, Joseph 83
DUSTAN, Jon 76 Jonathan 76 Jonathan Jr 76
DWIGHT, Capt 27
DWINNELL, Hezekiah 78
DYER, Stephen 84
EADEN, Edward 84 Thomas 84 Timothy 84
EADY, Samuel 79
EAGER, Soloman 79
EASTMAN, James 83 Samuel 76
EATON, David 76 Ebinezer 84 Thomas 76 William 83
EAYERS, Leut Coll 102
EAYRS, Coll 98 Leut 95 Leut Coll 97 99
EDMOND, Walter 84
EDWARDS, John 83 86-87 Joseph 84 Joshua 83
ELESLIE, Leut 93
ELFLAM, Andrew 84
ELIOT, Thomas 79
ELLIOT, James 83
ELLWILL, Hesediah 83
EMERSON, Edward 73 83 Moses 78 Thomas 73 83 86 87
EMERY, Edmund 79 Stephen 7
EMES, Phinias 84

EMONS, John 84
EMORY, Benjamin 84 Caleb 83
ENGENFIELD, Peter 78
ENGLISH, Joseph 79 Peter 76 Richard 84
ENLISTMENT BOUNTIES, 15
EQUIPMENT, 51
ESTEY, Benjamin 78
EVANS, 3 Henry 78 Simeon 79
EVELITH, Joseph 79
EVENO, John 84
EVESSON, Daniel 84
FARNHUM, John 84
FARRES, James 84
FARROW, Andrew 84
FAST, Jonathan 84
FAULKOSEN, Paul 84
FAY, Josiah 72 77
FELLOCK, Ebenezer 79
FELTON, Anthony 76
FENICK, William 79
FESSENDEN, Jonathan 77
FESSENEN, Jonathan 72
FIME, David 84
FISH, George 84
FISHER, Joshua 79 Timothy 79
FISK, Daniel 79 David 79 George 84 Isaac 84 John 84 Mark 76 Thomas 79
FITZGARALD, William 84
FLACK, Thomas 84
FLAG, Elisha 79 Enoch 79
FLAGS, 32 39
FLANDER, Joseph 79 Lewis 79
FLANDERS, 3 Enoch 79 Nehemiah 79
FLASKS, Tin 37
FLING, Morris 79
FLOTILLA 1758, 4 32
FLOYD, Andrew 78
FOLEMSBEY, John 76

FOOT, John 79 Samuel 76
FORD, Thomas 79
FORT EDWARD, 3 23 32-33 39 51 92
FORT MILLER, 39
FORT TICONDEROGA, 3 5 22 37 39 43 46
FORT WILLIAM HENRY, 3 5 23 35 51
FORTRESS LOUISBOURG, 5 7 48 55
FOST, Malachi 84
FOSTER, Abner 79 Benjamin 84 Ezekiel 78 Jonathan 79
FOWLE, Joseph 84
FOWLER, James 76
FOWLES, Benjamin 84
FRAIZER, Mark 79
FRANK, George 84
FRASER, Mark 84
FREEMAN, Joseph 79 Mathew 84
FRENCH, Jacob 78 James 76 84 Joshua 84 Moses 84 Sampson 84 Solomon 79 Timothy 79
FRENK, John 76
FROST, Silas 79
FRYE, Benjamin 84 Joseph 47 Simon 83
FULLER, Andrew 72-73 81-82 Archelous 73 82 Capt 93 Joshua 84 Josiah 79
FULTON, Joshua 84
GAGE, Coll 92 Maj 91 95 100
GAGES, Brig 99
GAITERS, 29
GALE, Abraham 73 77 81
GALEHAL, Abraham 83
GAMATT, Paul 76
GARDNER, Israel 76
GARLAND, John 84
GARLING, Joseph 79

GARRITT, Charles 83
GARUATT, Paul 76
GATES, Hezekiah 79 Oliver 79
GATT, John 84
GAVITT, Benjamin 76 78
GAY, David 79 Jeremiah 79
GEORGE, Capt 56 Gideon 79
   Samuel 71-77 79 81-82 86-87
   Samuel Jr 76
GEORGE, Lake 1 5 17 23 39 51-52
   91-102 -Lake Champlain
   Corridor 32 Battle of 3 27 31-32
   62
GETCHELL, Nathaniel 76
GETCHILL, Ezra 79
GIDDENS, Daniel 79
GISSING, GIDDINGE,
   GIDDINGS, Andrew 72-74 81
   82 86-87
GIEER, George 79
GILBERT, Col 32
GILBRISH, John 84 Jonathan 84
GILES, James 84
GILLISON, John 84
GILMORE, Nathaniel 76
GITERRMOR, Robert 83
GLAZER, Zachariah 79
GLAZIER, Bensley 71 75 77
GLEESON, Isaac 79
GLOVER, Capt 56 Edward 73 77
   Samuel 72-74 82 86-87
GODARD, Ens 94
GODFRAY, John 84
GODFREY, Joseph 79
GODWIN, Enoch 79 Michael 84
GOE, Joseph 76
GOIER, Bartholimew 76
GOLD, Benjamin 79 John 79
GOLDTHOUGET, John 84
GOLDTHWAIT, Jacob 79 Joseph
   82 86-87 Michael 79

GOLDTHWAITE, Joseph 71
GOOD, John 84
GOODALE, Benjamin 79
GOODMAN, Nancy 86
GOODRIDGE, John 79 84
GOODWIN, Joseph 81
GOOKIN, Samuel 79
GORDEN, Thomas 84
GORSWOOD, Maj 100
GOSS, Peter 79
GOSSLFORD, William 84
GOULD, John 83 Noah 79
GRANT, Coll 91 94 97-98
GRASET, Martin 84
GRAVES, Phinehas 76
GRAY, Daniel 84 Ephrum 84 John
   84 John Jr 84 84 Joshua 84
GREAT COATS, 35 47-48
GREEN, Darius 73 82
GREENLEAF, Daniel 84 Joseph 74
   81-82 Samuel 21 23-24 32 54
   72 77 79 Thomas 76 William
   73 83 86-87
GREENO, Ebenezer 79
GREPCOCH, Richard 83
GRIBWATTLDE, Maj 95
GRIDDING, Capt 56
GRIFFIN, Andrew 84 Ann 86
   Daniel 83 Jonathan 79 Mathew
   84
GRIGGINS, William 84
GRIMES, John 84 Moses 83
GRISWOLD, Maj 91
GRITS, Charles 84
GROSS, James 78
HACKET, 3 John 76 Theodore 76
   Thes 76
HACKIT, James 79 Theophilus 79
HADLEY, George 84 James 84
   Joshua 84
HADLOCK, Joseph 76

HAGGER, Daniel 84
HAIR, James 78
HALDEMAN, Coll 98
HALDEMON, Coll 95
HALDEMOND, Coll 92
HALDERMAN, Coll 101
HALE, Gershom 79 Robert 7
HALL, Abijah 78-79 Amos 84 John 84 Jonah 83 Stephen 84
HALLAFAX, 97
HALLIFAX, 92
HAMILTON, Marmaduke J 79
HAMMON, Edward 84 Richard 84
HANCOCK, John 78
HANDLEY, Thomas 83
HANNER, Capt 56 George 82
HANNERS, 86 George 72-74
HARBEY, Joseph 76
HARDING, William 79
HARDY, Joshua 79
HARKNESS, John 76
HARNOT, Jacob 84
HARRINGTON, Thomas 79
HARRISON, George 83
HARRISS, John 94
HART, 91 94 102 Coll 95 98-100 Ebenezer 76
HARTMAN, Matthias 79
HARTSHORNE, John 79
HARTWELL, Joseph 79 Solomon 79 Thomas 72 74 77
HARVAY, John 83
HARVER, Samuel 84
HARVEY, Dorothy 6 Jacob 76 John 79 Theophilus 79
HASHAW, Samuel 83
HASKELL, Stephen 78
HASTING, Andrew 79
HASTINGS, Benjamin 73 82-83
HAT, 27 30 32 35-36 47-48
HATCHET, 27 37 39 48

HATHAWAY, Guilford 84
HAVELAND, Coll 92
HAVERLAN, Coll 100
HAVERLAND, Coll 91 94 99 Gen 91
HAVERSACKS, 27
HAVILAND, Coll 96
HAVURLAND, Coll 93
HAWS, Samuel 79 Stephen 79 Thomas 76
HAY, John 76 Peter 76
HEARD, Nathaniel 76
HEATH, Jonathan 79 Joshua 84
HENDERSON, Waldo 73 83 86-87
HENSHAW, William 22
HERRIN, Ens 92
HERRON, Catherine 86 Edward 84 Niehemiah 84
HEWES, Elisha 74 83 86
HEWINS, William 79
HICKS, Abram 84
HIDDEN, Jonathan 77
HIDE, Benjamin 79
HILL, Abraham 79 Nathaniel 76
HILLERY, William 83
HODGDAN, Benjamin 84 Seamon 84
HODGEKINS, ---- 84
HODGSKINS, Moses 76
HOLDEN, Justinian 78 Sgt 55
HOLEGATE, Asa 79
HOLLADY, Francis 78
HOLLAND, Edward 79
HOLLIDAY, John 76
HOLMES, Christopher 79 Zebulon 79
HOLMON, James 84
HOLT, John 74 82 Samuel 84 Uriah 79
HOLTON, Jacob 84 John 84
HOOPER, Levi 84

HOPKINS, Edward 73 83 86-87
HORTON, David 79 Edmund 79
HOSKINS, Jacob 83
HOUGHTON, ---- 71 Elijah 77
   Timothy 72-74 77
HOVEY, Isaac 76 Joseph 79
   Thomas 79
HOW, Isaac 79
HOWARD, --- 83 Thomas 84
   Timothy 79
HOWLES, John 76
HOYT, Jacob 76 84 Mathia 76
   Samuel 84 Theodore 76 79
   William 84
HUBBARD, Peter 79 William 79
HUBERT, Abram 84 John 84
HUCHINGS, Joseph 84
HUCHINS, Benjamin 84
HUDSON, Darius 79 Eleazer 76
   Eliezer 76 79 Nathaniel 78
HUDSON RIVER, 51
HUGHES, Amuel 84 Samuel 84
HULTON, Amos 84 Samuel 84
HUMPHREY, Abijah 79
HUNT, 3 Edward 84 Ezekiel 79
   Moses 79 Nathaniel 76 79
   Phillip 76 Wm 79 Zebedee 79
HURGADER, Leut Coll 93
HUSSTIN, John 92
HUTCHINGS, Capt 55
HUTCHINS, Benjamin 79 Hesekiel
   71 77 Hezekiah 72 77 81
   Hezekial 73 82 John 79 Joseph
   84 William 84-85
HUTCHINSON, George 85 Israel
   73 82
IEWETT, Jonathan 85
ILSLEY, Joseph 73 82 Stephen 77
INDIANS, In Bagley's Regiment 10
   Stockbridge (Mohicans) In
   Bagley's Regiment 10

INGALLS, Abijah 85 Benjamin 74
   83 86-87
INGASULLE, Maj 97 99
INGERSOLL, 72 Benjamin 74
   Joseph 71-74 77 81 Nathaniel
   72-73 75 77 82
INGRAHAM, Abram 83
IRELAND, David 79
ISAAC, Follett 84
ISLEY, Paul 79
JACKET, 27 32 38
JACKIT, John 79
JACKSON, Joseph 37 85
JENKINS, Robert 76
JENKS, Capt 55
JESLING, Mathew 85
JESUIT, Joseph 82
JEWETT, Ezekiel 76
JEWITT, Thomas 76
JOHNSON, 3 Benjamin 85
   Dillington 79 Gen 1 3 51
   Hezekiah 79 Jonathan 78 Moses
   79 Nehemiah 79 Peter 78 81 Sir
   William 10 Timothy 83 William
   1 23-24 55
JONES, ---- 83 Jacob 79 John 76
   Samuel 79 Thomas 79 William
   76
JORDAN, Elijah 79 Samuel 79
   Thomas 79
JURSEY, 94
KEMP, Timothy 79
KENDRICK, James 79 Samuel 85
KENNEY, Nathaniel 79
KENNY, Jonathan 79
KENT, Daniel 79 Joshua 85
   Richard 80
KENY, Jonathan 73 77
KERN, Inow 85 Mathew 85
KETLER, Henry 85 William 85
KETTLE, 27 35-37 39 48

KEYES, Joseph 82
KIBLER, Jacob 80
KIDAALE, Mathew 85
KILTSON, John 85
KIMBAL, Thomas 76
KIMBALL, Benjamin 73 83 David 80 Edward 85 Thomas 80 William 76
KIMBLE, Asa 80
KINCHIN, John 80
KING, Ebenezer 85 Elisha 85 Theodore 85
KINGSALL, 91
KINGSBERRY, Benjamin 77 John 77
KINGSBERRY (KINGSBURY), Benjamin 72
KINGSBURY, John 71-73 75-77
KINNEY, Samuel 78
KLYNE, Philip 85
KNAP, Ebenezear 80
KNAPP, Mathew 83
KNAPSACKS, 27 33 35-39 48
KNIFE, 27
KNIGHT, Daniel 80 David 76 Ebinezer 82
KNOLTON, Ebenezer 76
KNORELTON, Thomas 85
KNOWLES, Thomas 90
KNOWLTON, Samuel 73-74 82-83 86-87
KNOX, John 47
L, Moses 85
LAGER, Stephen 85
LAKEMAN, John 76
LAKING, Oliver 37
LANABEE, John 48
LANE, David 80
LANTHORNS, 35
LASEL, Elison 85
LASH, Robert 85

LASKEY, Robert 85
LAURAMEY, Joseph 85
LAURANCE, Jonathan 80
LAWRANCE, Capt 37 John 85
LEATHERBY, John 85 Joseph 85
LEBBY, Samuel 85
LEDDEL, Henry 82
LEE, Nehemiah 85
LEGGINGS, 29 32 38
LEONARD, David 80
LEVISTON, John 80
LEWIS, Jabez 80
LEWITT, Ezekiel 78
LIDDEL, Henry 23 78
LIGHTS, 51
LIMBRICK, 99
LISCOMB, Ebenezer 80 John 80
LISLE, James 80
LITTLE, Moses 7
LONDON, 96 102
LONEY, Thomas 76 80
LONG, Edward 85 Sam'l 72 75 77
LONGLEY, Robert 80 Zachariah 74 82-83
LONGLY, Benjamin 85
LORD, James 85 John 74 83 Philip 73 75
LORING, Capt 51
LOUISBOURG, 62 *See also:* Fortress Louisbourg
LOUISBURGE, 91
LOUISBURGH, 95
LOUSE, William 85
LOUSIOYE, I 82
LOVEJOY, Ens 93 Isaac 74 82
LOW, Stephen 73 82
LOWATER, Stephen 76
LOWE, Nathaniel 76
LOWELL, 3 Eliphalet 80 Gideon 78 John 78 Jonathan 80 Moses 78

LOWWATER, Stephen 76
LOYD, John 78
LUDWICK, Jacob 80
LUSCOMBE, Richard 85
LYMOND, 94 102 Coll 98 101 Gen 95 99-100 102
LYNCH, Margaret 86 Michael 85
LYNCOLD, Elisha 83
LYNCOLN, Oliver 85
LYNDAY, Jonathan 85
LYNEAFOR, Jebadia 85
M'CLEROY, William 74 86-87
MACE, Bernard 80 George 76 80
MACHEM, Joseph 76
MAINE, Bagley's Purchase of Land In 6
MANGARSON, ---- 85
MANNING, Thomas 80
MANSFIELD, William 76 85
MARROW, Ebenezer 72-74 81
MARS, James 78
MARSH, Moses 78
MARSHALL, Anthony 85 Samuel 76
MARTIN, Isaac 73 82-83 86-87 Isaiah 80 Jacob 83 Josiah 76 Michael 73 83 86-87
MASON, Aaron 78 David 49
MASSACHUSETTS, Bagley's Purchase of Land In 6
MASSACHUSETTS-BAY, 19 23
MASSACHUSETTS-BAY COLONY, 63
MATHEWS, Silas 80
MAXFIELD, Joseph 80 Obediah 80
MAXWELL, Elijah 76 Hugh 80
MAY, Joseph 80
MCCLAIR, Mary 86
MCCLARAY, Daniel 85
MCCOMM, John 83
MCCOY, Alexander 80

MCCOYE, Abigail 86
MCDONALD, ---- 85 James 83
MCELROY, William 74 83 86-87
MCFADDEN, Francis 80
MCFIRSON, Margaret 86
MCFIRSON, William 85
MCGOON, Josiah 80
MCLEOD, Alexander 74 86-87
MCNAB, John 80
MCNEAL, James 80 William 80
MCNEALE, John 85
MEANS, Daniel 85
MEARS, John 83
MEDICAL CARE, 6 53 63
MEDICAL CHEST, 53
MEDICINE, 53
MERRATT, Jacob 83
MERRELL, Jacob 76 85 John 85 Moses 83
MERRILL, 3 Joshua 80
MERRIMAC RIVER, 6-7 9 13
MERSY, Leut Coll 92-93
MESSAY, Leut Coll 101
MESSER, Abiel 73-75 82
METOON, James 80
MIDLETON, William 83
MILLENDY, Richard 80
MILLER, David 85 George 85 Hezekiah 78 Philip 83 Stephen 71-73 77 81
MILLIKEN, John 80
MILWOOK, Mathew 85
MISNSTER, Maj 101
MISSEN, Ens 93
MITCHELL, Jonathan 85 William 76 80
MITCHIN, Isaac 85
MOFFITT, Joseph 85
MOGGARIDGE, 3
MOHICANS, 10
MOLTON, Elijah 80

MONEYPENNEY, Brig Maj 96
   Maj 92 94
MONEYPENNY, Brig Maj 98
MONKTON, Col 32
MOODY, Joseph 72 Joshua 73-74
   83 86-87
MOOR, Capt 91 93 Wm 94
MOORE, Benjamin 80 Capt 55-56
   Edmund 72 73-74 81-82 86-87
MOORS, Francis 80 Wm 92
MORGAN, Richard 80
MORGARIDGE, Samuel 80
   William 80
MORIAM, Thomas 82
MORISON, Bradley 78
MORRIL, Jacob 76
MORRILL, 3
MORRISON, Samuel 85
MORSE, Andrew 76 David 85
   Edmund 76 Elisha 85 Isaac 85
MOULLON, David 85
MOULTON, Johnson 73 83
MUGERIDGE, William 83
MUNROW, Dr 95
MUNTUSK, Philip 85
MURPHY, Edward 80 Thomas 85
MUSKETS, 31 36-37 39 48 52-53
NAST, Ebenezer 80
NECK COVERINGS, 29 49
NELSON, Ambrose 80
NEMENS, David 85
NEVERS, Samuel 80
NEWALL, Joseph 82
NEWBURY, Massachusetts 9-10
   13
NEWHALL, Capt 56 Joseph 72-74
   81-82 86-87 Richard 85
NEW HAMPSHIRE, 10 Bagley's
   Purchase of Land In 6
NEWLAND, Moses 80
NEWTON, Joshua 80 Richard 80

NEW YORK, 93
NICHOLAS, Aaron 80 William 80
NICHOLES, Joseph 76
NICHOLLS, 94
NICHOLS, Joseph 22-24 26 38 52
   60 Samuel 80
NICKOLL, Coll 99
NICKOLLS, 102 Coll 95 98 100-
   101
NICKOLS, Coll 91
NIKOLLS, Coll 95
NORCROSS, Isaac 80
NORTON, Jonathan 78
NOVA SCOTIA, 5 7 17 47 55
NOYCE, Ward 82 86-87 William
   76
NOYES, John 22 Jonathan 78 80
   Nathaniel 80 Samuel 85 Ward
   83
NUROSS, William 80
OBEN, Hezekiah 80
OBRIAN, Thomas 80
ODELL, Joseph 83
OFELAWAY, Joseph 85
OHERON, David 85
OLEMAN, John 85
ORMOND, Philip 85
ORR, John 85
OSGOOD, 3 Oliver 85 Samuel 80
   Solomon 80
OTIS, James 78
OTTEN, Leut 92
OWEN, Hezekial 85
PACIST, Josiah 80
PACKER, Bartolomew 80
PAGE, Abraham 80 Abram 83
   Ichael 85 Jonathan 76 Nathan
   80 William 85
PAGNETT, Joshua 85
PALINGALL, Samuel 83
PARKER, Benjamin 78

PARKER (Cont.)
  Jonathan 85 Joshua 82 Josiah 80 Zachariah 80
PARKMAN, Francis 27 32 37
PARLINE, 95
PARROT, Daniel 83
PARSONS, Jonathan 85 Phinias 83 Thomas 78
PARSSONE, Coll 100
PARTRAGE, Coll 100
PARTRIG, Coll 96
PARTRIGE, 91 94 101 Coll 97-99
PATCH, Nathan 77
PAUL, John 85
PAYSON, Leut Coll 92 97 Samuel 80
PEABODY, David 80 Francis 87 Richard 78
PEARCE, Joshua 82
PEARSON, Jonathan 73 75 82
PEIRCE, John 78
PELL, William 77
PENNY, John 80
PERKINS, Jacob 80
PERLEY, Benjamin 80
PERRY, Eliakim 80 Josiah 80 William 85
PERSEY, Israel 80
PETTINGALE, Edward 80 Joseph 80 Matthew 80
PHETLOCK, Michael 77
PHILBROOK, Mich 77
PHILBROOKS, Ephraim 80
PHILIPS, John 77 83
PHIMES, Asha 85
PICHMAN, Joshua 85
PIEKOLL, Robert 85
PIERCE, Jonathan 78
PIKE, ---- 85 Pearly 74 Pearly (Parley) 82 Thomas 71-72 75 Thomas Jr 77

PILBURY, Timothy 85
PILSBERRY, Msoees 80
PILSBURY, Elijah 80
PIPER, Nathaniel 80
PITT, William 38
PIXLEY, Aaron 80
PLUMER, William 83
PLYMOUTH, 97
POGONIT, Joseph 80
POLAND, Francis 77
POMEROY, 27 32 Seth 24
POOL, Benjamin 85 William 80
POOR, Enoch 22 73 83 86-87
PORTER, Daniel 74 82
POTTER, Anthony 78 Robert 76 Samuel 80
POWDER HORNS, 33 36 39
POWERS, Jonas 80
POW WOW RIVER, 6 13
PRAINGER, Joseph 85
PRATT, ---- 85 Eleory 85
PREBBLE, 99 Coll 94 98 100-101
PRESBY, John 77 80
PRESON, John 77
PRESSEY, Moses 77
PRIBBLE, 91 Coll 94-95
PRICHARD, Eli 77
PRINCE, Moses 74 77
PROCKTER, Jonathan 85
PROCTER, Josiah 82
PUFFER, James 80
PULVER, Jeffry 77
PUNHAM, Pitt 80
PUNISHMENT, 59-60
PUSSEY, Moses 77
PUTNAM, Amos 76 78 Asaph 80 Henry 83 Joseph 83
RAG, Robert 80
RAMSDELL, Ephraim 80
RAN, Hanniniah 80
RAND, John 80

RANDKER, Enoch 85
RANDLE, David 85
RANGERS, 91 95-98 100-101
RATIONS, 18-21 23-25 32-33 60
　Bagley's Table 25 Officers' 24-25 Supplements To Soldiers' 21
RAY, William 85
REA, Caleb 21 53 82-83 Dr 53-54 59
READ, George 85
REALY, Charles 80
REATHINFORDS, Capt 91
RECRUITMENT, of Family Members 15 Procedures 15
REDCOATS, Provincials Feelings About 62
REDDINGTON, Samuel 83
REED, Elijah 80 Isaac 85 Samuel 73 83
REGIMENTALS, 30 47
RELIGION, 59
REMICK, Isaac 78 Joseph 78
RENNELDS, James 80
REYNOLDS, James 77
RHOADES, Jonathan 85
RICHARDSON, Amos 22 Binson 85 David 85 Stephen 77 Thomas 85 Winston 85
RICHMOND, Elisha 83
RICKER, Zerah 80
RIGATT, John 85
RIGGES, David 77
RIGGS, Daniel 80 David 77
RIPTERS, Dennis 85
ROADS, Samuel 80
ROAHDEY, Andrew 77
ROBBINS, John 80
ROBINS, Richard 82
ROBINSON, Elijah 80 Oliver 80
ROBISON, Josiah 80
ROGERS, 94 John 85 Jonathan 80

ROGERS (Cont.)
　Maj 95 97 Robert 10 Samuel 80 83 Stephen 85
ROGERS RANGERS, 99
ROSE, Joseph 78
ROUNDEY, John 74 83
RUGGLES, 47 Timothy 23
RUNELLS, Samuell 72 75
RUSSELL, Richard 80
RUST, Walles 86
RYONS, Henry 85
SAWYER, Benjamin 80
SAFFORD, Abra 77
SAINT LAWRANCE, William 83
SALISBURY POINT, Massachusetts 7
SAMSON, Daniel 78 Joseph 80
SANDERS, Edward 80 Humphrey 80
SANDERSON, James 82
SARGENT, Stephen 71 77 81
SATCHELL, Jeremiah 80
SAUNDERS, Benjamin 80 Thomas 76
SAWING, James 80
SAWYER, J 82 Richard 80
SEACHELL, Jeremiah 77
SEAKES, Edward 77
SEAMONS, James 85
SEARLETH, Numan 85
SEMONS, William 77
SERGANT, Josiah 74 77 Thomas 77
SERGEANT, Charles 78 Philip 78 Zebediah 80
SERGENT, Stephen 72-73 75
SERJANT, Samuel 77 Treworthy 77
SERJEANT, James 77 Phillip 76
SESSIONS, Josiah 80
SEVER, Moses 80

SEWALL, Dummer 74 83
SHACKFORD, Sumner 80
SHAPOSE, John 85
SHARP, Catto 85
SHAW, Daniel 85 John 85
SHEAFF, Edward 83
SHEAFFE, Edward 86
SHEETS, 35
SHEPARD, Daniel 80 John 80
SHIPWRIGHTS, 3 13
SHIRLEY, William 35
SHIRTS, 27 29 32 35 37 47-49 55
SHOES, 27 30 35 37-38 47-48 62
SHOOTINGS, Accidental 53
SHORDWONT, John 85
SHORTWELL, Margaret 86 Richard 85
SHOULDER KNOTS, Yellow 47
SHRAGGUE, William 85
SIMMONS, Robert 83 Thomas 83 William 83
SINKLER, John 80
SKIDMORE, Richard 83
SLAP, Maj 99
SLAPP, Maj 94
SLINGS, 31 35
SLOOPS, 15 51
SLOPS, 29
SMALL, John 77 80
SMITH, Abram 85 Arron 85 Ballard 80 David 80 85 Ebenezer 80 Henry 85 Hesakia 85 Jacob 76-77 80 John 80 85 Jonathan 85 Joseph 80 Richard 83 Samuel 76-77 Seth 80 Solomon 85 Walter 85 William 76-77 Zebediah 80
SNOW, Ebinezer 83
SNOWFORD, David 85
SNOWTIAL, William 85
SPALFORD, David 82

SPANDERS, Hiah 85 Jonis 85 Mary 86
SPANISH INDIAN, In Bagley's Regiment 10
SPAULDEN, Josiah 80
SPEAR, Benoni 80
SPENCER, Maj 96 101
SPITTLE, Brig Maj 97 Maj 93 101
SPOONER, Carl 85 Ruggles 80
SPOONS, 35
SPRAGUE, Jonathan 82
SPRING, Elisha 85 Thaddeus 78
SPRINGFIELD, 100
SPYWOOD, Thomas 35 80
STANWOOD, Jonathan 85
STAPLE, Ebenezer 85
STAPLES, Samuel 80
STARDIFNE, Church 85
STARDIFNT, Isaac 85
STARNS, E 82
START, George 80
STAYDEN, Daniel 85
STEARNS, Phineas 80
STEELE, Jonathan 85
STEELYARDS, 35
STEPHANS, William 85
STEPHENS, ---- 83
STEVENS, Nicholas 78 Thomas 72 77
STICKNEY, Samuel 85 Solomon 80
STINSON, James 85
STITES, Joseph 83
STITES, Bernard 85
STOCKBRIDGE MOHICANS, 10
STOCKER, Robert 80
STOCKINGS, 27 29 32 35 37-38 47-48
STOCKMAN, 3 Joseph 80 William 78
STOCKWELL, Samuel 80

STOFER, John 85
STOKER, Robert 85
STONE, Henry 78 John 85 Josiah 85 Robert 85
STOTON, Maj 95
STRAW, Gideon 78
STREETER, Joseph 80
STURDITON, Robert 83
SUCKERS, Joseph 82
SULIVA, Joseph 80
SULIVAY, Jonathan 80
SULIVY, Daniel 78
SURGEON, 10 17-18 21 24-25 33 53
SURGEON'S CHEST, 53
SURGEON'S MATES, 10 17-18
SUTTON, Margaret 86 Robert 85
SWAIN, Jonathan 77
SWAN, Samuel 80
SWEATS, William 22
SWEET, Moses 80 Samuel 80
SWETT, 3 Benjamin 73 75
SWORD BELTS, 60
SWORDS, 32
SYDAR, John Henry 85
SYDEN, John 85
SYKES, Richard 73 82
TALBOT, Amaziah 80 Daniel 80
TAPLEY, ---- 71 77 Samuel 80
TAPLIN, Capt 10 37 John 71-75 77 81-82
TAUNT, William 80
TAYLOR, Samuel 85 Seaman 85 William 73-74 76 78 82-83 86-87
TEMPLE, Francis 73 82-83
TENCA, Elisha 85
TENTS, 31-33 38 49
THOMPSON, Alexander 82 Jacob 83 Margaret 86 Nathan 76 Rebecca 86 Samuel 77

THOMPSON (Cont.)
Thomas 78 Timothy 85
THOMSON, Edward 80
THORNTON, Ann 86 Gilbert 74 77
THORP, Moses 85
TICKOMB, Maj 96
TICONDEROGA, 1 32 51 Battle of 37 *See also:* Fort Ticonderoga
TIMEY, Oliver 82
TIMOTHY, David 85 Etisha 86
TINDER, Benjamin 83
TINGLERS, William 85
TITCOMB, Col 3 David 72 81 Maj 92 101 Moses 1 3
TOGG, Seth 85
TOLIN, Mathew 85
TOLINSBURY, John 77
TOOTHAKER, Andrew 85
TOSS, Thomas 85
TOUPEN, Benjamin 83
TOWNSEND, John 85 Jonathan 86 Richard 80 William 85
TRAFTON, Charles 76 Zachary 77
TRAIN, Joshua 80
TRAINING, DRILL, EXERCISE, 52
TRANSIER, Esekial 85
TRASK, Jacob 85
TREBUE, Francis 85 Hanah 86 Mary 86
TREDWELL, Samuel 82
TROUSERS, 47
TROUGHT, William 85
TROWBRIDGE, Thomas 74 82
TRUCK, Jacob 77 80
TRUE, Bradbury 85
TRUMP LINES, 27 37-38
TUBBS, Daniel 85 Lourana 86
TUCK, Samuel 85
TUCKER, Daniel 72 77 John 85

TUCKER (Cont.)
    Joseph 80 Uriah 78
TUCKERMAN, Abraham 73 83
    86-87 Isaac 73 83 86-87
TUPPER, Simeon 80
TURNER, Abner 80 James 77
TURRELL, Josiah 85
TUSK, Daniel 80
TUTLE, Samuel 77
TUTTLE, David 83 John 85
    Samuel 77 85
TUXBURRY, Henry 85
TWINEY, Leth 85
TWIST, John 85
TWON, Francis 80
TYLER, Jacob 87
UNIFORMS, Clothing In General
    62 Officers' 36-37 47-49
UNIFORMS 1755, 27 29 33 38 49
UNIFORMS 1756, 36
UNIFORMS 1757, 36
UNIFORMS 1758, 37
UNIFORMS 1759, 48
UNIFORMS 1760, 48
UPHAM, Jabez 80
VARNY, Benjamin 83 Joseph 85
VINSENT, Thos 92 94
VOSE, Lemuel 78 Seth 80
W, John 85
WADE, Ichabod 85 Samuel 85
WADLEY, Moses 85
WAGES, 6 14 17-19
WAGONS, 1 21 33 35 52
WAISTCOATE, Benjamin 85
    Thomas 85
WAISTCOATS, 29-30 35-37 47-49
WAKEFIELD, Benjamin 85
WALE, Niles 86
WALKER, Benjamin 86 Nathaniel
    80 William 86
WALLINGFORD, Samuel 80

WALLIS, Jacob 86
WALTER, William 80
WARD, Josiah 82 Nicholas 86
WARE, Michael 80
WARNER, John 86
WARREN, Jonathan 80
WARTHIN, George 77
WATKINS, Phineas 80
WATSON, Pelatiah 80
WAYMAN, Jonathan 80
WEBSTER, 3 Capt 51 Samuel 80
    Stephen 71-72 74-75 77
WEED, John 80
WEID, Elemaleck 77
WEIDE, Serjent 77
WELK, Enoch 80
WELLMAN, Silas 80
WELLS, Dorothy 6 Enoch 80
    Joseph 80-81 Nehemiah 86
    Phillip 81 Rev 6 Samuel 81
WENTWORTH, Sion 81
WEST, Elias 81 Jason 86 Maj 91
    93-94 96 Maj Coll 97
WESTFIELD, 101
WEST INDIES, 6
WESTON, Joseph 81
WESTWORTH, Silas 86
WETCOMB (WHITCOMB), John
    81
WHALE BOATS, 51
WHEELER, Ebenezer 77 Jonathan
    86 Peter 78 81 William 81 83
WHEELLER, Peter 77
WHEELRIGHT, Josh 86
WHEELWRIGHT, Daniel 74 77
WHICHER (WITCHER), Morrill
    78
WHIGHTING, 94
WHILLIER, Green 81
WHIPH, Ebenezer 77
WHIPPELL, Stephen 72-73 82

WHIPPELL (WHIPPLE), Stephen 82
WHIPPLE, John 75 Stephen 71-72 74-75 86
WHITAKEN, James 83
WHITCOMB, 3 Abel 81 Asa 71 73-75 82 Col 21 John 39 77 Leut Coll 93 97 101 Levi 81-82 Robert 82 Silas 81 William 78
WHITE, Hayfield 86 Philips 72 75 William 86
WHITEING, Coll 91 95-96 98 100 John 76 78
WHITING, Coll 99 Leonard 73
WHITING (WHITTNEY), Leonard 82
WHITNEY, Jonas 78 Jonathan 82 Josiah 81 Nathaniel 86 Salmon 72-74 82
WHITTEN, Joseph 81
WHITTING, Amos 86
WHITTINGTON, Joseph 81
WHITTOM, Joseph 81
WHITWELL, William 77
WHORD, Leut Coll 93
WHTMORE, Jonathan 81
WIBB, Mary 86
WIBBOR, John 86
WIER, Richard 82
WIGHTING, 102
WILDER, Jonas 78
WILLABOR, Henry 86 Joshua 86
WILLARD, 23 32 Abijah 20
WILLES, Andrew 86
WILLETT, Daniel 81
WILLIAMS, 91 101 Ames 73 83 Coll 93 96 98-99 Ebenezer 81 86 Elhaniah 86 Ephraim 32 Jonathan 86 Joseph 86 Samuel 74 77 Silas 86 Simeon 77
WILLIMANS, Coll 98

WILLINGTON, Thomas 81
WILLIT, Daniel 77
WILLSON, Barnabas 81
WILSON, Michael 81
WING, Thomas 77
WINGATE, 3
WINGET, Edmund 81
WINSLOW, Col 32 35 Gen 51 John 48
WINSTON, Isaac 86
WINTWORTH, Mathew 86
WISE, William 83
WISHER, Morrell 81
WITCOMB, John 78
WITHENELL, Solomon 86
WM, 94 Coll 95 100
WOMEN CAMP FOLLOWERS, 55 59 62 Bagley's Louisbourg 56 Bagley's Ration To Men 56 Bagley's Unit Relatives 56 Early War 55 Late War 55 Pay 55
WOOD, John 78 Sippie 77
WOODBERRY, Caleb 74 83
WOODBURY, Andrew 77 Elisha 78 Isaac 77 Josiah 74 83 Richard 81
WOODMAN, David 82 Moses 86
WOODS, John 81 Joseph 82
WOODWARD, Stephen 77
WOODWELL, 3 77 Gideon 71-72 75 77 Rubin 83
WOOL, John 86
WOOLFORD, Martin 81
WORCESTER, Oliver 81
WORMS AND WIRES, 27
WORTHEN, Ezekiel 81 Jonathan 81 Joseph 78
WORTHIN, George 81
WORTHY, George 78
WOSTER, 94 102 Coll 91-92 95 97-100

WOTEN, John 86
WOTHIN, George 72
WRIGHT, Jonathan 86 Nathan 86
   Oliver 37

YOUNG, Abraham 81 Abram 77
   Benaiah 71-72 75 77 Gideon 86
   Joshua 81
ZACHERY, Isaac 81

www.ingramcontent.com/pod-product-compliance
Lightning Source LLC
Chambersburg PA
CBHW070500100426
42743CB00010B/1707